The Digest Book of

RACQUETBALL

ob Gura

Follett Publishing Company / Chicago

T-1421

Credits and Acknowledgements

Instructional Photography
Bruce and Caren Schulman

Models
John Lynch—1979 Illinois State Racquetball
Association Men's Singles Champion.
Glenda Young—1979 Illinois State Racquet-
ball Association Women's Singles Champion.
Joan Rogers—"A" level competitor.

Cover Photography
Art Shay

Court Facilities
**Spaulding Racquetball Club—Lincoln Park,
Chicago, Ill.**

Associate Publisher
Sheldon L. Factor

ISBN 0-695-81421-4   **Library of Congress Catalog Card #79-91653**

TABLE OF CONTENTS

CHAPTER 1

The Name of the Game

CAN YOU NAME the fastest growing sport in America? Here's a clue: if you opted for football, baseball, or basketball, guess again. The same goes for tennis, gymnastics, or water skiing. Maybe this'll help. Unlike the others it's played behind closed doors (one to be precise).

No, it's not handball, but you're on the right track—the name of the game is racquetball. Like handball, racquetball is contested in a large box-like room immune from the elements.

In addition to similar battlegrounds the two share other common bonds. Each makes use of a small rubber ball which is vigorously pounded about varying combinations of walls. Each can be played by individuals or paired teams. Both sports utilize the same scoring structures, and set equal limits as to the length of a game.

There are however, several distinct differences. Handballers employ a ball constructed of hard rubber, racquetball uses a softer orb. Handballers propel the ball with a swat of callus-covered palm. The other uses a highly refined hitting aid.

It wasn't always that way though. Prior to racquetball's appearance, individuals wishing to partake in the pleasures of handball but reluctant to bruise the flesh were forced to use wooden paddles.

While the paddles were somewhat heavy to handle, they added some interesting highlights to the game. Struck with a layer of wood as opposed to skin, the ball (a somewhat softer version) tended to move faster, and rebound farther. As such, paddlers were able to make increased use of the ceiling and backwall.

It took a while for this radical deviance to catch on. By 1950 however, paddleball, racquetball's forefather had become established.

Human nature being what it is man (and woman) seeks to constantly find ways to hit the ball a little harder, play the game a little faster.

One day in 1950, in Greenwich, Conn., a man named Joe Sobek provided the next link along the developmental road. A squash and tennis teacher by trade, Sobek longed for a method by which paddleball could be improved as a teaching aid. Pondering the problem

one day, a moment of divine contemplation came upon him. If the wooden face of the paddle could be replaced with tension strung nylon a la a tennis racquet, the game would be radically altered. The power of the new device would be vastly superior to the paddle. It would also be lighter, hence there would be less of a fatigue factor as play wore on.

Designed to the exact weight and length of the paddle the new kid on the block was a hybrid personified. Half-paddle half-tennis racquet, it came to be known as a paddle-racquet.

For almost two decades the new game virtually be-

The modern racquet has evolved from humble beginnings.

The creation of a professional racquetball circuit has helped showcase top caliber in action across the country.

came the exclusive property of a small coterie of West Coast adherents.

While the paddle-racquet (or PR) lived up to its expectations, participants were initially caught in a quandry. Should the rules of handball, or tennis, or squash, or a combination apply?

Having formed the Paddle Racquet Association shortly after the paddle-racquet's inception, Sobek sought to solidify the sport by formulating the rules and promoting the game.

With the passage of years the new sport began to prosper. Finally, in 1969, a watershed moment arrived. Participants gathered together and decided to hold the first national tournament. Both the players and the sport were in readiness. All that remained was to settle on the name of the game.

After much deliberation a monicker was chosen which pleased all concerned. The label was racquetball, and it has become the fastest growing sport around.

By latest estimates more than 5 million men, women and children participate nationwide in over 2,000 facilities. The game is played across the country, with new courts springing up in each day in different regions. Major nerve centers of the sport are San Diego, St. Louis and Chicago.

Persons in search of discovering the joys of racquet-ball needn't strain their vision to find a court. New facilities are being erected each month by private entrepreneurs and such organizations as athletic clubs, YMCA's, Jewish Community Centers and more than a few colleges.

Ever since that first tournament a decade ago, racquetball has seen a steady growth in numbers. With the creation of a professional circuit in the early 1970's the sport has been able to showcase top-quality players in action across the country. Along with such other factors as the fun of the game and its capacity to be played in all weather, the pro stars helped broaden an already growing appeal.

At the time of the 1969 tourney (held at the St. Louis Jewish Community Center, by the way) the International Racquetball Association (IRA) headed up by Bob Kendler was established. Kendler, a long time father figure for handballers remains equally active today in the world of racquetball.

Operating under the guidance of various administrative bodies racquetball continues to flourish today on both amateur and professional levels. Newcomers to the game can rest assured they're entering into an activity which has not yet neared its peak in popularity. According to all forecasters the outlook for the sport is bright, and should remain so into the foreseeable future.

CHAPTER 2

Why Racquetball?

NEWCOMERS TO THE GAME would be hard put to relate racquetball to other American athletic staples.

Unlike the basic team sports there is no physical contact permitted, and the court is three-dimensional.

Individuals used to grassy playing fields, cement floors or large stadiums may find the dimensions hard to relate to.

Like a stranger in a new land they may glance about in disbelief on the first trip to a racquetball court.

Judged on appearances it's easy to see how first impressions could be puzzling.

The object of the players' attentions is a small black (or red, green or blue) rubber ball bounding ferociously off any combination of walls and ceiling.

The seemingly sawed-off tennis racquets used by the participants would also pique the curiosity.

If the picture of two or four people pounding a ball about a room 40'x20'x20' to no apparent purpose doesn't seem strange enough, the sound effects verge on the surreal.

Each time ball meets racquet a "thupping" sound ensues, followed by an eerie "tharumphing" when ball meets wall.

In between the thupps and tharumphs the players add to the melody. With each shot sounds of inhalation and exhalation can be heard, punctuated by occasional rasps or sighs of relief.

With each stoppage of play (for reasons to be explained shortly) the participants usually either shout encouragement or heap verbal abuse upon themselves.

Tiring of the exercise they usually emerge from the box, shake hands and depart amicably.

If the overall impression fails to cause the newcomer to wonder, a snatch of post-match conversation should prickle the curiosity. Where else but from a box-like room where shots echo would such terms as Z-ball, garbage serve, rollout, and half-lob be accepted terminology?

For many individuals the joining of a unique playing field with diverse action and a singular lexicon are too much to bypass. When it's realized the game itself is a world of fun and exercise, another player has been hooked.

Although the majority of individuals reading a text on the sport are concerned with various strokes and strategies there's a whole other world to ponder. You may not have stopped to consider, but racquetball lends itself easily to conviviality and pleasant relationships.

For many people in fact, the weekly racquetball session and time spent afterwards has become part of a rewarding social ritual.

Many facilities are aware of this high sociability quotient and plan accordingly. After a brief workout it's not unusual to see a pair of competitors relaxing and chatting over drinks in a comfortable lounge. In addition to racquetball, most clubs offer a host of additional diversions such as whirlpool baths, saunas, exercise equipment and television.

Regardless of whatever calls you forth it's nice to know the opportunity to meet and greet new friends and business associates in pleasant surroundings exists. Anyway you look at it, it sure beats sitting home on a rainy day.

By the way, racquetball clubs are terrific places for singles to mingle and couples to get together. Many clubs will sponsor various specials and theme parties designed to increase esprit de corps (and boost attendance no doubt).

That sounds great, but there's another aspect to be aware of. Most clubs offering the facilities above are privately owned and are intended to make a profit.

Rates for play are roughly $12 an hour for prime time (generally from 3:30 PM - 10 PM) and less for other hours. Compared to the cost of a movie, it's no bargain. Then again it beats the entry price for many other social activities. There's generally an annual membership fee tacked on anywhere from $40-60 per individual. Price breaks on family memberships are normally available. The usual racquetball season runs from September to June so that's when clubs are most lively.

In case you're interested in following up the idea, here's a possibility. Pay a visit to your neighborhood club or clubs. Most will gladly allow you to sample their facilities free of charge or at a special rate.

Readers should be aware that excellent racquetball courts are available at YMCA's, Community Centers, and other public facilities. Since these organizations offer racquetball as an adjunct to their total programs fees are often quite less.

So, whether you're a newcomer or observer give it a try. By the way, dieters, an hour of racquetball burns away over 300 calories. You can have a good time while ridding the frame of some excess baggage.

Oh yes. Don't forget the kids. Children of all ages are flocking to racquetball. Many clubs have heard the cry and provide special classes for their instruction.

After watching a fast-paced game few newcomers could fail to be impressed by the speed and seemingly joyful confusion of racquetball.

With each shot the ball caroms off walls, different each time in speed and direction. The players move at angles across the court, seeking to anticipate the direction of an incoming shot while gauging their own return.

Sometimes the action is brutally swift, with a service return failing, and a point quickly won. Other shots bore in straight and true, low on the wall. Bouncing twice before the opponent can reach the ball, they register an easy win.

Not all shots pack the power of a knock-out punch; some are intended only to tease and deceive.

Batting the ball high off the ceiling a player will often force the opposition to retreat to backcourt for a difficult return. Rather than risk a tough rally-ender the hitter will return in kind, and wait his opportunity. The chess game will continue for several shots with each participant on the lookout for an error.

The moment a shot returns weakly off the wall the opponent is on it like a fox sighting a rabbit. Before the foe can blink twice the return has rocketed by, a sure winner.

"It looks exciting, but can I hope to play like that?" the novice might ask.

The answer is encouraging. Of course you can. All it takes is a little bit of practice and then some.

One of the great strengths of racquetball is despite the speed and diversity of shots it remains one of the easiest sports to master.

The basic fundamentals of the game can be readily understood during the first session. A pair of newcomers can enjoy a mediocre though albeit invigorating match first time out. The quality of play will be raw at best, but from a competitive standpoint the contest could be up for grabs.

And why are the fundamentals so easily grasped?

Simply expressed, racquetball is a simple game to play. All things considered, it's definitely harder to hit a baseball, shoot a basket, or throw a football than it is to hit a ball against a wall.

The basic mechanics of hitting a racquetball are aided by the tremendous force generated by the nylon strung racquet. Even a totally untutored, quasi-coordinated individual will be able to deal the ball a punishing blow.

Of course there's a great deal more to the game than

Many racquetball clubs offer convivial atmosphere and the convenience of an in-house pro shop.

just smashing the ball about the walls at will, but it's a fine place to be able to start.

Best of all, most everyone is capable of stepping forward and joining in the fun. Whether the object is to compete at a tooth and nail pace, enjoy a leisurely game, or simply meet some new friends, racquetball supplies the means.

The game offers a panorama of sporting thrills. From the rally-ending finality of a roaring, low shot off the front wall (called a kill), to a cerebral, high-bouncing ceiling ball, the player can participate to his arm's delight.

And 5 million people can't all be wrong. Of that a startling number of women are represented. Since racquetball offers the privilege of play at varying skill levels, the machismo present in other sports is largely absent from the game.

Women, men and children of varying skill levels can enjoy being matched against and practicing with players of their caliber. As such, these individuals participate with a heady sense of competitive fervor, as victory is most always within reach.

Regardless of whether you're man, woman or child, young, old or older, racquetball has something to offer. The only thing left to do is step on court and recreate.

CHAPTER 3

The Rules of the Game

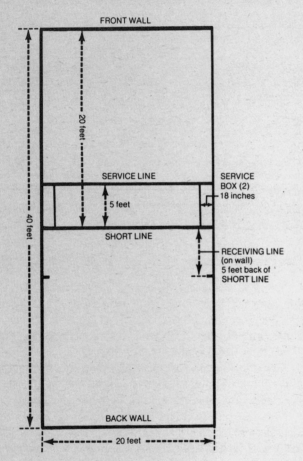

FRONT WALL

20 feet

SERVICE LINE

SERVICE BOX (2)
18 inches

5 feet

SHORT LINE

40 feet

RECEIVING LINE (on wall) 5 feet back of SHORT LINE

BACK WALL

20 feet

RACQUETBALL IS PLAYED within the boundaries of a court 40 feet long, 20 feet high and 20 feet wide. The boundaries are easily noted because they're walls; generally made of plaster or concrete painted white. Occasionally specially constructed glass is utilized as it permits greater visibility for spectators.

The walls serve as more than boundaries. Except in certain instances (to be explained shortly) the side walls, ceiling and back wall are all considered playing surfaces.

The playing court has a series of lines (red or white) painted on the wooden floor. More than enhancing the color scheme, these lines serve the vital function of deliniating the field of play (see diagram).

One of the lines, dubbed the short line, stretches across the court at a spot 20 feet from the front wall. It only takes a quick glance to establish the handy reference point provided by the short line. It divides the court in half. It follows that the area in front of the short line is called the front court. Space behind the short line is the backcourt. Five feet in front of the short line, 15 feet from the front wall, another line spans the floor. This is the service line. The space between the two is the service zone. Each time the ball is put in play the server must stand within this area.

Racquetball is played in a court 40 feet long, 20 feet high and 20 feet wide. Diagram (above) and perspective drawing (right) give dimensions and names of the principal parts of the court.

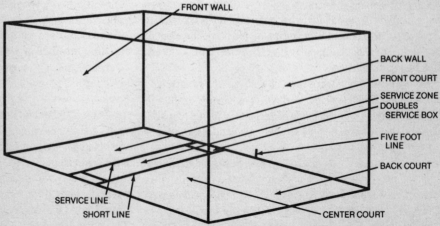

FRONT WALL

BACK WALL

FRONT COURT

SERVICE ZONE

DOUBLES SERVICE BOX

FIVE FOOT LINE

BACK COURT

SERVICE LINE

SHORT LINE

CENTER COURT

Server's foot must not extend beyond service zone lines.

The Serve

Play begins with the server holding the ball somewhere within the service zone. He or she has up to 10 seconds to serve. This feat is initiated with the server bouncing the ball on the floor. Contact must be made on the first bounce. The ball must then strike the front wall. It must rebound past the short line prior to hitting the floor. If the ball fails to pass the short line before striking the floor it is termed a short, similar to a fault in tennis. Two consecutive fault serves result in a loss of service, called a "hand out." A sure no-no. Enroute from the front wall the ball may contact one of the side walls before touching the floor. If however, before it touches the floor, it strikes two side walls or glances off the ceiling or back wall it is considered a fault. As with faults concerning the short line, any combination of two service faults results in loss of service.

The server can lose the serve without a second attempt at a legal serve if: the ball strikes the floor, ceiling or a side wall *before* striking the front wall. This is termed an "out serve." Other out serves can occur when the server swings and misses the ball in serving, and when the ball, on rebounding from the front wall, touches the server.

Assuming the serve is good, that's when the fun begins. Despite first impressions all the frenzied running and ricocheting is goal oriented: the object being to score points.

The Return

The key to success is the ability to return every shot to the front wall on the fly.

Whereas the server could not strike the ceiling or back wall with the serve, the returner is not burdened with such restrictions. He or she is given license to strike the ball off any combination of walls enroute to the front wall. In order to deliver a "good" return, however, there are several guidelines to observe. First, the returner must hit the serve before it bounces on the floor twice (yes, it's legal to hit a serve without it bouncing first—more on that to follow). Secondly, the return shot cannot bounce off the floor prior to making contact with the front wall. Any time that happens it's called a skip ball.

If the return stroke is good, participants take turns hitting the ball until one player commits an error.

These miscues take two forms: either the shot strikes the floor before hitting the front wall or a player cannot hit the ball before it has bounced on the floor twice.

Whenever one of these two events takes place, or the server faults twice on the serve or out serves, the rally is ended. A rally by the way is the time the ball is kept in play until a winner is hit.

Scoring

Play continues until one player reaches a total of 21 points. Unlike tennis, points can only be scored at the service line. When the server loses the rally the score remains the same, but service changes hands.

In case you're wondering about the similarity with tennis, there's another important difference. Whenever the score reads 20-20, the next point won terminates play. Due to this absence of "deuce," the intensity prior to play of the final point can be mind-boggling.

Matches are generally played on a best-of-3 basis. The match winner is the first side to win two games. In the case competition is so even each athlete wins a game, a tie-breaker is played. This takes the form of an 11- or 15-point contest, winner take all.

This rule strives to ensure every point of every game is played with total intensity. It's important for each player to not only win each game, but to score as many points as possible. This offensive vigilance can pay off in a big way when the first two games are split. When the tie-breaker arrives the player who scored the most points overall will be awarded the service.

At this time, note the existence of the two boxes located at opposite ends of the service zone (see court diagram). They're called service boxes, and measure 18 inches from the side walls. As far as singles play is concerned, forget about them unless you appreciate their symmetry. Their sole function is reserved for doubles. They mark where the non-serving partner stands until the serve passes the short line.

The Safety Zone

Other court markings worth noting are two short vertical slashes evenly aligned along the side walls. No, they're not the addition of a line-painter grown weary anointing the floor. The lines, 5 feet behind the short

A screen ball occurs when the serve rebounds off the front wall and passes close to the server's body—it is considered a dead ball serve and is replayed without penalty.

The server must also abide by the rules. Following the service the server cannot retreat until the ball has safely crossed the short line—to do so is a service fault. Although hardly noticeable, the receiving lines have proven well worth the paint cost in terms of band-aids, bruised tissues, or worse.

One more rule worth heeding for both novices and veterans is that of screening the ball on the serve. This occurs when the ball rebounds off the wall and passes close by the server's body. Since the body impedes visibility, the service must be re-played. Once again, it's based on the view of prudence before flair. A returner unable to see the service is likely to make an inaccurate return or a flesh-seeking shot.

It's helpful to keep a few key points in mind:

Point 1. When serving, the ball must strike the front wall first, and rebound past the short line.

Point 2. The service can strike one of the side walls on the fly after contact with the front wall.

Point 3. The service may not make contact with the back wall or ceiling during the flight of the serve.

Point 4. Any time the serve fails to comply with these criteria, a fault is awarded. Two consecutive faults result in the loss of service.

Point 5. Points are awarded only on the service.

Point 6. A rally is concluded when a hitter is unable to return a shot before it bounces twice, or the ball bounces before hitting the front wall.

When the time comes you're ready for that first step on court it's vital to remember courtesy counts.

line and 3 inches high are there for a vital purpose. The motivator is called safety first, a principle which necessitates the need for these "receiving lines" and the "safety zone" they create.

Being the hard fought game it is, competitors are prone to rush into battle with racquets blazing. Nowhere is the temptation to smite the ball as intense as during the return of service. In order to ensure neither returner or racquet make contact with the server, the receiving lines are installed. The returner cannot move forward of this line until the ball has been served and has passed the short line. A recently-introduced rule change now prohibits the receiver from *striking* a return of serve on the fly in front of the receiving line. Either violation by the receiver results in a point for the server.

The Most Common Service Errors: 1) Serve hits ceiling after striking front wall—a fault serve. 2) Serve fails to pass short line before hitting the floor —called a "Short Serve", it's a fault serve. 3) Served ball hits two walls on the fly after first striking the front wall—a "3-Wall Serve", it's also a fault serve. 4) Serve hits sidewall, ceiling or floor before hitting front wall—an "Out Serve." 5) Serve hits backwall before touching floor—called a "Long Serve," it's a fault.

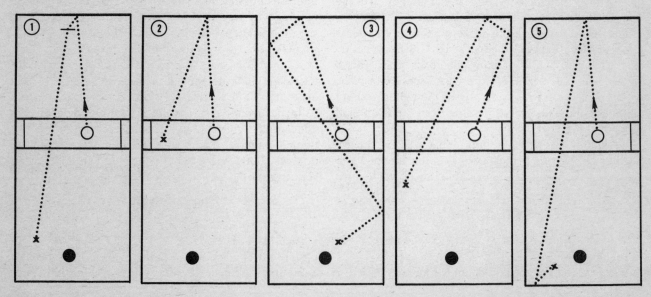

An avoidable hinder from two perspectives—it results in an out or a point depending on whether offender is serving or receiving.

The Hinder

Racquetball is an extremely fast-moving game played within regulated confines. As such, any contact between racquet, ball and body should be avoided.

There's little doubt a racquetball whizzing about court can resemble a rubberized comet. The velocity of the meteor can be misleading. A major league pitcher can hurl a fastball to the plate at speeds upward of 100 m.p.h. A professional racquetball player can rocket the ball forward 40 mph faster. It may not hurt as much or as long, but it still stings.

It doesn't require an overly developed imagination to picture the painful reunion occasioned by rubber meeting flesh.

In order to minimize the number of these instances the sport has instituted an effective counterbalance. It's called a hinder and goes far toward alleviating the problem.

Keep in mind while a referee will announce violations during a tournament, most players will serve as their own judges. Therefore honesty must be the best policy.

There are two varieties of hinders. They are the avoidable and unavoidable. "What!" you may burst out. "Why would someone deliberately hinder a player." Well, it often happens, especially in doubles.

What might surprise you is the penalty inflicted if the referee thinks the hinder could have been avoided. If you guessed the loss of the rally you're right again.

It's rare for casual players to call avoidable hinders though, so let's check out the everyday unavoidable variety. Each time one is called, the point will be replayed.

According to the rules there are six types of unavoidable, or "dead ball" hinders. The first example listed under regulation 4.10(a)(1) concerns an unlikely occurrence—the court hinder. It states the rally will be replayed if the ball hits any part of the court considered out of play. "Now what part of that box-like court could possibly be out of play," you ask? Think about it for a moment. How about the light fixtures, door knobs, hinges, or any cracks or warped walls? Then again, a competitor could jam a towel or loose ball can into one of the corners. Although it's an unlikely occurrence, the rule helps curtail many an otherwise vehement argument.

Rule 4.10(a)(2) deals with a subject we've already mentioned, the unwanted union of ball and body. Any time a returned ball touches an opponent on the fly (before the ball touches the front wall), the rally will start again from scratch. Any veteran player or newcomer who has ever been "touched" by a hard hit drive has reason to snicker at the regulation's delicate wording. Take it from legions of racquetballers, "touch" could more properly read "smacked."

Moving on we come to 4.10(a)(3). This aspect is designed to preserve life and limb. Any bodily contact with the opposition interfering with the ball being seen or hit is considered a hinder. This refers to situations when a player unavoidably makes body contact while

An unavoidable "Dead Ball" hinder resulting from body contact that interferes with ball return.

racing toward the ball. It also entails those moments when a player is forced to pull up short before hitting the ball due to the presence of the opponent.

Anytime you feel there's a good chance you'll hit your opponent with either ball or racquet, stop and shout "hinder." Not only will you feel better for the deed, but your opponent will respect the courtesy.

The fourth stricture, Rule 4.10(a)(4), has to do with the relationship between the ball and body. Namely how close the former can pass by the latter. These hinders are concerned with the proximity between a ball rebounding off the front wall and the player that hit it. If the ball passes near enough to interfere or prevent the return the call will be made. Take note, remember this ruling applies to serves, also. Doubles players heed the following. Any serve passing between the server's partner and the side wall will also be considered a hinder. Don't laugh, some players have been known to try it.

The fifth facet, Rule 4.10(a)(5), concerns players with an acrobatic bent. It's the straddle ball, which relates to players attempting airborne gyrations. It's called anytime the ball is obscured passing through the legs of members of the hitting team. Although it may seem unlikely, even sedentary players have been known to execute the maneuver in the heat of battle.

Finally comes the catch-all rule—4.10(a)(6). It covers any other unintentional interference which prevents the opponent from seeing or returning the ball. This could relate to the floor cracking, an electric blackout, or whatever.

There's one other application which is also interesting—especially for newcomers. Any time a player is about to make contact with another during the backswing, he or she should immediately call hinder. This is the only time a player has final say on the ruling.

Rule 4.10(d) is dedicated to the proposition all doubles players are entitled to a free and visually unim-

paired chance at returning the ball. This rule is interesting in that it applies when a player is hindered in the pursuit of a ball enroute to a teammate. The hinder is called even if the partner has already begun the approach for the return. Oh, yes, hinders only concern members of opposite teams. Although many newcomers effectively hinder the progress of their partner they'll receive no succor from the official.

Having studied the unavoidable let's move on to the more costly "avoidables." There are three major variations on the theme, each resulting in the loss of the rally for the offender.

The first penalty is inflicted when a player fails to move sufficiently to allow the opponent a clear shot—Rule 4.11(a).

Another is an offshoot of the above, but slightly more devious. Whenever a player moves into a position that blocks an opponent about to return the ball an avoidable hinder will be called—Rule 4.11(b). This violation is difficult to detect in doubles. The call is made when a player moves in front of a member of the opposition as his or her partner is about to return the ball. Beginning doublers should take extra care to note this restriction. During the battle for position, newcomers often disregard the opposition. Unfortunately, they also have a right to exist. The best way to avoid the blocking trap is to check the opposition's position before rushing in headlong.

The avoidable hinder is also assessed whenever a player moves into the way and is pelted by a ball played by the opponent—Rule 4.11(c).

This application is one of the more controversial strictures in the game. Regardless of talent level, many players feel whenever the call is against them, it's just plain wrong.

This view is prefaced on the notion each player is entitled to his own space. Therefore, if no one has been blocked out, how can the call be made. It's a sticky wicket, especially when contrasted with the unavoidable hinder 4.10(a)(2). If you recall, any returned ball hitting the opponent on the fly before striking the front wall will be replayed.

Hawk-eyed readers will be able to discern the rationale between losing the point or having it replayed. It's that old bugaboo, intent. And one thing for sure, it's hard to locate a player who'll admit guilt on the issue.

The best advice beginners can receive is identical to what was dispensed above. Always try to be aware of the opponent's whereabouts before pressing forward—especially in doubles.

There's one more occasion which necessitates an avoidable hinder. Fortunately, the majority of players have little reason to worry. The call is made when a player deliberately pushes or shoves an opponent. Hopefully few players will be so moved to forcibly bully their opponents on court.

The hinder, both avoidable and un-, is just one of a

group of regulations players should be aware of. Some concern procedural matters, others like the hinder are action-oriented. Even cursory knowledge of these no-no's and how-to's should help improve your play. Many readers may wonder what happens when the ball cracks or splits. Does it make a difference who hit the ball, or whether the fractured sphere can be returned? Not a bit, according to regulation 4.9(g). If the referee decides the ball is broken or otherwise defective (usually dead-bouncing) a new ball will be put in play and the rally replayed. "Okay," you say, but what if you're not convinced the ball is playing up to par. Perhaps it's too lively, dead, or lopsided. In that case, inform the referee. Any time between rallies either the ref or players can ask for an inspection. If the referee feels the bouncer isn't up to snuff it'll be tossed out and a new ball brought in.

Sometimes embarrassing events take place on court. A shoe lace may come untied, sweat band collapse over a limp wrist, or a shoe may fall off. Anytime a player loses a piece of equipment or a foreign object enters the court, good old 4.9(h) comes to the rescue. The moment the referee notices the loss or entrance, play will be stopped. Of course, the player can always bring notice through a spoken word or verbal outburst (hopefully not). The rule also contains a provision for play to be stopped if outside interference occurs. With any luck the appearance of either foreign objects or alien visitors will be infrequent at best. It's nice to know, however, the rulesmakers foresaw the possibility of UFO's. Then again, a racquetball court is an unworldly appearing structure.

Know the Basics

Before setting feet oncourt, it can be helpful to go over some of the basic essentials. The following can be found under Rule 1 of the U.S.R.A.-N.R.C. regulations for those interested in detailed study. To begin, racquetball can be played with two or four people (although, off the record, there's an entertaining three-person version called cut-throat). Games are played to 21 points with the first to reach the mark landing the kudos. These most generally take the form of handshakes and a free drink among friends.

Now it's time to review some of the game's more heinous infractions. The majority of these lamentables have to do with the service. Each of the following translates into a "side out" or loss of service.

Without a doubt they rank one and two on the list of the most desired avoidables. First, make sure every time you serve the ball it hits the front wall first. There is absolutely nothing as mortifying as stepping up to the service line, coiling your body like a spring, and hitting the floor with the ball. A close second is the pitiful sight of the ball leaping off the front wall and colliding with the server's body. Some feel this is the more grievous miscue. While in the first instance the service was sim-

A "Court Hinder" will be called if the ball should happen to strike the towel in the corner.

ply off-target, the second bespoke a lack of shot selection, physical grace and awareness.

The other service errors worth avoiding are less costly, but equally desirable to purge from your game. Faults are awarded anytime a serve strikes either the ceiling, two side walls or the back wall after contact with the front wall. If the ball lands in front of the short line after bouncing off the front wall the rule will also be enforced. Commit any two in a row and walk directly to the backcourt. Then hope your opponent gets overconfident and repeats the procedure. The player also must relinquish the serve upon taking more than 10 seconds to serve.

You can also surrender the service by delivering a deft stroke towards the ball and missing entirely. It's very difficult, however, to swing and miss a ball bounced by your own hand. Therefore, it seems likely the causal factor is something other than profound physical ineptitude. Most of the time the name of the villain is that old warhorse, nervousness. Beginners are much more prone to flail the air at the service line than are experienced players.

There's only one remaining variation of self-flagellation that can transpire on the service. Although it sounds physically distressing in nature, rest assured the crotch serve will only cause mental anguish.

"What, a crotch serve?" Yes, and it's no joke to servers who have fallen victim.

Before going any farther into what must seem a fringe area, a crotch is the juncture, or meeting place of any two court surfaces.

Places to avoid on the service are the areas where the front and side walls meet.

However, a serve that heeds a proprietous path off the front wall and lands in a backwall crotch is considered in play.

Besides smacking of the illicit this serve is a sure winner, as it's duty bound to bounce wildly after impact.

Now that we've noted the harbingers of doom concerning the service, it's time to blow the smoke from some blurry areas.

If, in doubles, the service strikes the server's partner in the service box the point is not lost. Whenever this event takes place it is called a Dead Ball serve and is replayed. Other transgressions such as the aforementioned screen ball or unavoidable court hinders are also considered dead ball serves. Those interested in pursuing the matter can devour rule 4.4, sections a, b, and c.

Some Odds and Ends

Leaving the service and it's pantheon of possible perils behind, let's shift to a totally different concern. Here's a question. Give yourself one ego boost for a correct answer. You're in the midst of a tightly played doubles match, when a drive comes screaming towards your partner. Stretching towards the ball he or she takes a lusty swipe at the ball and misses entirely. Positioned behind your partner you notice the miss and watch the ball move in your direction. Gathering your wits together you swing and hit a low kill to win the rally.

Here's the question. Was your shot legal?

Choice A: Yes, because the ball was never touched by your partner.

Choice B: No, because only one member of the team is allowed to swing on a return.

Choice C: No, but the pair of swings was sufficient to hinder the opponents' sightlines. The point will be replayed.

Tricky, huh. Well if you chose B, good try but no cigar. The same goes for C.

The correct choice is A, and bears testimony to the value of never taking anything for granted. Many times players have a tendency to relax (in doubles) when they see an easily returnable shot heading towards their partner. While the chances are unlikely you'll have to deal with the prospect, it makes sense to keep your eyes wide open. A constant state of readiness is a great asset on the racquetball court. Any game played on a four-walled court with numerous individuals milling about is prone to unexpected events.

Oftentimes the team better prepared to cope with a weird bounce or stroke will come away the winner—for many players there's no such thing as too fine an edge.

Another question in the mind of many beginners, especially ex-paddleballers, is "can I change hands?" For these unacquainted with paddleball, the hitter is allowed to switch the paddle from hand to hand on any stroke. The benefits from this practice are obvious. An individual cursed with a weak backhand can totally eliminate the stroke from his or her repertoire. At the same time, the use of a forehand on the backhand side allows an easier and longer extension when it comes to stroking the ball.

This procedure is taboo, spelled in capitals, in racquetball. While the thought of purging the need for the backhand undoubtedly has merits, no one has figured out a safe way to do it. In order to switch hands players would have to grip the racquet without the wrist thong in place. This ommission would give birth to an epidemic of identifiable aluminum and fiberglass aircraft. One thing for sure, it'd take some doing to locate a player willing to serve as a landing strip.

Still, the search goes on for an acceptable alternative to the backhand. If necessity really is the mother of invention some player plagued with backhand woes will discover an answer. Until then remember to use the hand with the wrist thong attached to hit the ball.

Tennis players interested in taking up racquetball wonder whether or not a two-handed backhand or forehand is legal. Choice A: Yes. Choice B: No, the point is lost. Choice C: No, the point is replayed.

Two-handers, rejoice. The technique is totally permissible. Due to its ever widening popularity in the net game, more and more beginning racquetballers are using the double grip.

Although it's legal, common sense rules against. Tennis players use two hands for increased leverage when gripping the longer handled racquet.

A racquetball racquet, however, is small handled and doesn't require the extra boost. Use of the two-handed grip actually serves as a deterrent, robbing the stroke of added extension and momentum.

One final point concerning the rules. Many courts are structured with a spectators' gallery atop the back wall. In many clubs the back wall stops at about 15 feet to provide a clear view of the proceedings. There are few players who haven't hit a smash off the front wall that became a souvenir for a lucky fan.

When this happens the point is replayed. The players may or may not get their ball back depending on the courtesy and footspeed of the recipient.

CHAPTER 4

Weapons and Battle Array

SO, YOU'VE DECIDED it might be fun to try your hand at the sport but don't know exactly what racquet to grasp.

It's an important issue to be decided, and there are no few choices to select from. Far and away the most important piece of equipment for play or practice is the racquet. Manufacturers are aware of this fact of court life, and have responded in the marketplace. A first visit to the sporting goods store in search of the sword of your dreams can be a mind-boggling odyssey with racks upon racks of racquets differing in materials and styles.

First, a word about racquets in general: According to the rules laid down by the U.S.R.A. the racquet can have a maximum head length (that's the part that smites the ball) of no more than 11 inches. The width cannot exceed 9 inches; the handle, 7 inches in length.

When the numbers are put together the total length and width of the racquet cannot exceed 27 inches.

Have no fears about the small dimensions. A top-ranked pro can power a racquetball well over 140 mph, with many regular club players able to approach the century mark.

There are two reasons the ball (to be discussed shortly) can be directed in such a rapid fashion. They have to do with the relatively low weight of the racquet and the tension with which the nylon strings are wound.

While racquets vary in size, most tend to weigh between 280-290 grams. Males tend to use the heavier versions, but that's by no means a hard and fast rule.

In case you find it hard to measure in grams, think in ounces, between 8½ and 9½ in most situations.

The nylon strung between the length and width of the racquet face is of key importance when it comes to packing a punch.

Most people purchase racquets which have already been pre-strung by the manufacturers. These racquets tend to be strung with between 22-30 pounds of tension.

When it comes time to decide whether to go with the high or low tension, remember the following rule-of-thumb. The greater the tension the greater the power, and the lesser the control. While the power generated by the increased tension is readily understood, the issue of control could use further explanation. Control refers to the degree of directional accuracy attainable in propelling the ball off the racquet face.

The longer the ball remains upon the strings the greater the chance for accurate placement and lower string tension allows longer ball contact. Debate continues to rage in informed circles over which tack is best to pursue. Many newcomers and professionals opt for

Racquets, either aluminum or fiberglass, come in a dazzling array of shapes and colors; in addition choices of handle size and grip material are offered.

the high tension route, enjoying the ability to plaster the ball. Others prefer greater control with less tightly wound strings in the 20-22 lb. area.

Fiberglass vs. Aluminum

Racquet construction falls into two basic materials: aluminum and fiberglass. The majority of players agree on one point. Fiberglass racquets tend to offer more control than the aluminum variety. Due to their increased flexibility or "give," the hitter enjoys a maximum of control.

As always, however, for every asset there's a liability. Inasmuch as fiberglass framed racquets are nowhere near as durable as their aluminum counterparts, they tend to expire at an earlier date.

Beginners should be wary of this fact when making their purchase. Newcomers are apt to swing overhard or wildly at first; hence the chance for imminent destruction upon contact with a sidewall.

Once the ability to swing without tattooing the wall has been established, the fiberglass avenue may be the route to pursue.

Lest lovers of aluminum frames feel spurned, several verses praising the metal frame are in order.

For truly enjoying the feel of blasting a hard shot downcourt, the aluminum racquet cannot be touched. With string tension at about 25 lbs. the hitter also possesses a considerable amount of control and feel.

Individuals in the process of beginning their court careers would do well to remember the durability of the aluminum frame. It's difficult to render terminal damage to a metal frame in the midst of a set-to with a side wall. It follows the racquet tends to endure longer than its fiberglass counterpart.

As far as tension is concerned, readers should keep in mind Newton's law that for every action there is a reaction. Following up on that principle, it can be deduced constant pounding with a ball moving at high speeds can cause even the tightest strung string to give a little.

Therefore, in order to avoid undue loss of power (roughly 2-4 pounds of tension from the battering), it's wise to have your racquet restrung every few months.

However, there's no reason to immediately remedy this depreciation of tension. Keep in mind the adage regarding tension and control, and rejoice. While you may have suffered the loss of some power, you're gained that much more control. If, however, you happen to be (or know someone who is) a bruiser of the first order, racquets can be restrung at relatively low cost.

The next facet of racquetry you may be concerned with is that of the grip. A question immediately springing to the front is, "how thick a handle should the racquet have?" Most racquets come equipped in one of three basic handle sizes. They are small (4⅛ inches), medium (4⁵/₁₆ inches), and large (4½ inches). Some manufacturers produce models with grip circumfer-

Varying handle sizes for different hand sizes are on the market—here a woman's model.

ences as small as 3⁵/₁₆ inches for pint-sized palms. When making your selection keep in mind most women and youngsters are well served with the 4⅛-inch model. Individuals with average sized hands will do well with the medium grip.

It's difficult to gaze at the rows of racquets and not notice the varying shapes of the heads. Some seem rectangular, others rounder, and more uniform. Like all sports, racquetball provides an opportunity for manufacturers to individualize the appearance of equipment. Technically speaking, racquets are produced in four styles, oval, rectangular, quadriform or tear-shaped. While some may feel a preference for a certain style, the average player need not worry about it. Each model is designed to perform well in competition. When choosing the racquet of your choice you may or may not feel a preference towards a certain style. If you do, and all choices are equal, go with it.

Otherwise rely more on factors such as weight, comfort and ease of handling. One more point, those attractive mountings along the edge of the rim on aluminum racquets provide more than visual appeal. They're safety bumpers installed to provide a little extra protection in the ongoing battle with the wall.

Vibrations at the point of contact also play a role in the selection process. Some believe the aluminum racquet offers a larger sweet spot (area of maximum power) than fiberglass, hence it vibrates less. A rabid segment of fiberglass devotees believe the opposite to be true. They state fiberglass "gives" more on contact, imparting more than power to the swing. The essence of the argument boils down to the general belief that in aluminum there's power, in fiberglass control.

Before purchasing, apply the following test to all racquets under scrutiny. Place the palm of your racquet hand around the handle. Shake hands with the handle and look at the circle created by your thumb and index finger. If the space between the index finger and thumb is large enough to accommodate another finger the handle is too large. On the other hand (excuse the pun), if the index finger and thumb overlap, the handle is probably too small. Look for the happy medium where your hand closes comfortably about the handle. The ideal relationship will reveal the thumb and index finger barely touching each other.

Grip Materials

Okay, you've tried on a bevy of racquets and have narrowed the search to a final few. The weeding-out process which follows can be critical to your playing career. While several of the racquets feel fine when gripped, the handles may be covered with different materials. Some of the grippers will be composed of rubber, while others are leather. A few may claim to be made of space-age materials. A word to the wise: steer clear of Skylab models. Great debates have been known to ensue over which offers the most advantage, rubber or leather.

For the purposes of the general player (and pros also) the issue is simply a matter of personal preference. Rubber grips offer a good "feel" but tend to get wet and slippery from perspiration. This moisture factor is really nothing to worry about. A quick wipe with a hand towel will remedy the problem.

Leather grips are comfortable to hold, and seem to elicit a more substantive feel than rubber. Price could prove a prohibitive factor, however, as leather tends to cost more than rubber.

After the selection process has largely run its course the moment will arrive when you choose your weapon for the racquetball court.

While many individuals tend to make their choice only after arduous screening others are more easily pleased. The author knows several women, his wife among them, who chose to consider purchasing only racquets with blue frames. Fortunately for the bank account the blue models were nowhere as expensive as some red and yellow ones hanging nearby.

Before making the final purchase, try to play with a like model beforehand. Now, of course, few merchants are so altruistic as to allow potential patrons trial runs with unpurchased racquets.

The solution is to try out a sample model at your local club. Many clubs have pro shops that will loan or will let you experiment with varying racquets at little or no cost.

In case you don't have such facilities at your convenience, talk to some racquetball playing friends. If you enjoy at least tolerable relations they may be willing to let you try theirs out, or at least offer some advice.

Before the greenbacks are laid on the sales counter, however, listen closely. Racquets range widely in price these days. Generally speaking a totally competent racquet can be had for anywhere between $15-$35. "Now hold on a second," you're likely to say. Just the other day you sighted some real beauties at a sporting good store selling in excess of $50.

No one could doubt the accuracy of your observation. The important thing to remember is that few if any of these racquets are capable of playing the game themselves. And that's what they'd have to do to justify their inflated purchase price. By the way, there are racquets retailing for as much as $150.

Any number of name brand racquets (Leach, Wilson, Ektelon, Omega, etc.) can be had within the $15-$35 price bracket. So, unless you have champagne tastes, stay within a ceiling of $35 or so. When it comes time to buy a racquet stay away from wooden framed models even if they're priced under $10. "Why," you ask, "don't they play well?" Yes, they do, if you can find a court that will allow their use on the premises. Wood frames are objects non grata on most facilities due to their proclivity to splinter upon contact with a wall.

One thing to check when purchasing a racquet, and an important one at that, is a guarantee. Most manufacturers guarantee their frames against damage for a year, and strings for 90 days.

Use Wrist Thong

A final point concerning the purchase and use of your new racquet. That funny piece of string looped to the bottom of the handle is there for a vital purpose—the safety of yourself and others. Dubbed the wrist thong, it's imperative that every player keep the loop draped around his wrist during play or practice.

Hands tend to lose their grip under the strain of extra effort and the absorption of perspiration. On those unfortunate occasions when the racquet bids adieu to its holder, grim harvests can quickly be reaped. A flying racquet is one of the most fearful sights to be witnessed on a racquetball court. In addition to possible physical injuries certain mental ailments can take place. For starters, an end to invitations to play and a lack of post-match smiles from opponents.

Assuming you're interested in purchasing the racquet of your dreams, remember the following:

1. Make sure the racquet feels right in your hand.

2. Check to see the index finger and thumb barely make contact when gripping the handle.

3. Decide whether or not you need a fiberglass frame for control or an aluminum frame for power and durability.

4. Check the price range of the racquet and look for a name brand and guarantee.

5. Try out a selection of models before purchasing.

After the tedious and somewhat tortuous process of racquet selection has been completed, more deliberation lies ahead.

What to Wear

The topic for this round of debate is sartorial splendor, or what style of clothing you choose to wear on court.

As racquetball caters to the play of individuals, the sport offers an arena for the individual to express him or herself in terms of fashion.

Like any sport practiced by millions, the dress of today's players runs the gamut from cro-magnon to Beau Brummellesque.

It's up to each individual to pick the particular styles, but the necessary items are as follows.

The well turned out player will wear: sneakers, socks, gym shorts, a short sleeved shirt, and various accessories.

Starting from the bottom up, which is only fair since the feet undergo a heavy pounding, let's examine footwear.

Anyone who has ever recreated will attest—if your soles feel poorly the whole soul suffers.

Few sports cause participants to pound the pavement (or floorboards) as much as racquetball. During the course of a well-played match a player can expect to log well in excess of 2 miles.

In addition to straight out running, the game requires plenty of quick stops, twists and turns. Every now and then, players will find their feet leaving the floor as they dive in pursuit of a flying ball.

Don't let the thought of possible foot problems be a burden. The problem can be easily averted with the purchase of a trusty pair of sneakers. Virtually any name-brand sneaker will provide proper ankle and arch support with a maximum of comfort. Sneakers vary in price, but a reliable pair can be had anywhere between $10-$30.

Many styles of sneakers abound on the market, several of which seem more designed for space flight than court wear. Don't be misled by claims that mercurial speed will become yours simply by donning a specific brand of footwear. The rule to follow is simple: make sure the sneak fits comfortably, is neither too loose nor snug, and offers good arch and ankle support. As far as ankle support is concerned, any ankle twisters reading this should give some thought to the high-top style of sneaker.

"Not that ugly thing," you may say. Judged solely on appearance, it's difficult for adherents to boast of the high top's contribution to high fashion. If the need exists to protect the ankles though, high tops are the answer. Although some may feel the presence of ankle-climbers destroys their fashion appeal, the safety factor more than compensates for the loss.

Before stuffing the toes and other members into the sneakers, don't forget socks. Blisters are one of the worst nuisances that can befall a player. By wearing a snug fitting pair of cotton socks and sneakers, the fric-

A complete racquetball outfit: T-shirt, shorts, sweatband, socks, sneakers, balls, glove, racquet.

tion between skin and sole that causes blisters can be eliminated. Some players, however, are especially prone to incurring these nasties. A solution that comes to mind involves doubling the footwear. No, I don't mean two pairs of shoes. If you have severe problems involving blisters put a second pair of socks on over the first. The additional material inside the sneaker will help eliminate chafing action that leads to the dilemma.

Assuming the footwear issue can be settled with few qualms it's time to move on to a pithier area, that of shorts and shirts, or (in some cases, dresses for women) and accessories.

Any prospective player would be hard put to deny racquetball is a game of stark contrasts. Played within the confines of a white- or glass-walled room, players stand out sharply.

Many couldn't care less how they look, and their appearance proves it. It's easy to pick out this segment of the racquetball playing community. Just look for a dismally grey tee-shirt, somewhat riddled by holes, that appears to have been worn by three generations of the same family.

The shorts will offer graphic evidence of random

Inexpensive sweatbands for head and wrists sop up excess perspiration, make play more comfortable.

Clothing manufacturers are aware of the wishes of many players to look as sporty as possible. Therefore new lines of apparel designed for racquetball are appearing on the market each day. Virtually every outfit looks great; unfortunately the prices can be every bit as high.

All avenues considered most players choose a modified John Doe look. They don everyday tee-shirts and shorts but spice up the image with contrasting or complementary colors.

Whatever the choice, it's hard to overlook a player's appearance on court. So dress comfortably, and remember, you may never know who's watching.

Other articles of clothing worn by players are wrist and head sweatbands. These cotton strips are designed to sop up excess perspiration, but they also contribute visual appeal. Most are brightly colored and quickly catch the eye of spectators.

Purchase more than one in any case. Since they're used to blot perspiration the material can quickly become saturated. It's nice to have a spare to take over the salty duty. These bands are relatively inexpensive. A set of two can generally be had for under $3.

Just in case you're wondering when does all the regalia end, there's still more clothing to be considered.

Regardless of your temperament, it's hard to locate an individual who will deny perspiration under stress. Well, no matter how much pleasure you derive from playing, the body strains during the activity. As such, a certain amount of perspiration is bound to trickle from or down to the hand and palm.

Once the wet stuff comes in contact with the handle of the racquet the likelihood of slippage increases. This slippage can result in a loss of grip which cannot help play. While in some rare instances the hand may actually release the racquet, most times the consequences are merely irritating. The player, fearing the racquet hand is not in full control due to the dripping, may overreact. This can lead to wiping the handle after every volley, or eventually changing racquets. For many the answer is the racquetball glove. Most gloves are made of leather and feature either deer or calfskin palms with some form of terry cloth backing.

Do these gloves do the job? The answer is an unqualified yes, by all means. Does that mean you should run and purchase a few of these items? Not quite.

While there's near-unanimous agreement that the gloves do a yoemanlike job of absorbing perspiration, there are other factors to consider. Some say the glove distracts from the "feel" of the racquet. Others believe the gloves are unduly bulky. However, if you suffer from blisters they're virtually mandatory. As with sweatbands, buy a couple and experiment. By the way, they also tend to become sweat soaked quite quickly.

Before we leave the topic of garb a quick mention of the unmentionables is needed. Regardless of how low an esteem you guys may hold your athletic prowess, it's

contact with a washing machine. The feet will be covered with threadbare sneakers, offering a fleeting glimpse of the players' little toes. Concerned only with playing the game and little else, the clutch of players in this population are not reknowned for post-match socializing.

Moving up a bit from these sartorial neanderthals we can consider the John Does of the court. Members of this species are drawn towards clean, freshly washed shorts and shirts with few distinguishing features. Following dictates of both common sense and comfort the gym shorts fit snugly but not too, and the shirt follows suit. These players wisely choose cotton for the makin's of their garments and receive the benefit of the airy fabric. If you want to make an absolutely smashing appearance on court follow the lead of the Does but add a few embellishments.

These take the form of matching shirt and short outfits, adorned with stripes or other eye-catching vehicles. Women of course can apply the same standards if they opt to wear a tennis-type skirt and blouse, or dress. (Keep in mind, gals, the majority of players prefer the shorts and shirt route.)

Protective eyeguards or goggles (above) are a wise precaution. Eyeglass wearers should opt for shatterproof prescription glasses with safety strap. Racquetballs (right), available from several makers, come in a rainbow of colors.

a certainty enough strain will be exerted to justify wearing an athletic supporter. Personal preference is up to you but be sure whatever jock you choose fits firmly.

For you gals, be sure to wear appropriate support bras if you feel the need.

By the way, many players tend to wear sweatbands and gloves for another reason.

Sometimes an individual feels stronger or more confident wearing these items although he or she may never yield a drip of perspiration. As the old saw goes, "Every little bit helps."

Since we've been discussing excess moisture and how to best combat it, don't forget the simplest, most direct remedy of all, the towel. Or in the case of oncourt use, a half-, or small towel.

Just take a towel, tear or cut it in half and tuck one end into the waistband of your shorts. Located within easy reach, you'll be able to avail yourself of its services at any time. One thing to be careful of however: Be sure to attach the towel in a place where it won't interfere with play. Experiment a bit, and you're sure to find a safe harbor.

The ability to locate the ball quickly is a great asset, and one in which attentive eyesight plays a strong part. Since racquetballs tend to wizz about at terrific speeds and varying angles, it's wise to wear a set of protective, plastic eyeguards.

"What, those ugly things, I wouldn't be caught dead wearing them," you say. There's a lot to be said in behalf of your argument. Most eyeguards tend to impart a Martian-like appearance to the wearer. But, and it's a strong one, would you rather look otherworldly or suffer a painful injury?

Another argument offered against the eyeguards is that they restrict peripheral vision (the outer part of the field of vision). While several years ago this may have been the case, today's eyewear has largely surmounted the charge. The basic problem encountered by the be-goggled is getting accustomed to wearing the darn things.

Once you spend enough time to become acquainted with the eyewear you should find they're no trouble at all. And they can sure do a lot of good from the standpoint of prevention.

Now that you've chosen a racquet and clothing it's only fair to spend some time with the ball you'll be stroking.

Racquetballs are made of rubber, pressurized and packed two a can. In case you've never seen one before, or seen one and wondered what it is, glance at the photo. They certainly do resemble miniature tennis balls without the fuzzy covering. Those interested in the vital statistics should listen closely.

The ball is 2.05 inches in diameter, and weighs roughly 1.4 ounces. If you really want to stump your friends ask them how high the ball should bounce from a 100-inch drop at 76 degrees. No kidding, these are actual procedures prescribed by the U.S.R.A. and N.R.C. The answer to how the ball should bounce: between 68-72 inches.

One point worth noting is that a player can never own too many racquetballs. Despite the vigilance of the regulatory bodies and manufacturers (by the way the U.S.R.A. and N.R.C. use Seamco 558 and 559 balls) the balls seem to either lose their bounce after a few sessions or split on contact.

Don't frown at any other balls you happen to see on the shelves however. Both organizations reserve the right to deem any other brand sufficient as long as it conforms to regulations. The first or next time a ball splits following a strike you've delivered, there's no reason to despair. Sure the ball may have ruptured due to faulty design. Then again perhaps you simply overpowered it.

CHAPTER 5

The Proper Grip and Stance

ALTHOUGH RACQUETBALL may look like an exercise of protracted agony from the spectator's viewpoint, the participants are concerned with finality. Racquetball is a taxing sport physically. As such the players hope to win every rally as soon as possible. The game makes use of a wide range of shots, some specifically geared toward that end. Before a player can hope to end a rally with either a pinch kill or rollout, however, it's beneficial to understand the principles behind the shots.

Even the most myopic observer cannot help but notice the basic delivery systems that send the ball forward.

Regardless of the shot, odds are the ball was stroked with a variation of either the forehand or backhand. Since most individuals are more accustomed to use a forehand type motion (throwing a ball, casting a fishing rod, etc.) let's look at the forehand first.

More than any other facet, the forehand forms the foundation of a player's game.

The stroke constitutes the favorite means (except for a few cases) by which a player will hope to terminate a rally.

The forehand is the saberstroke of the player's arsenal. Armed with a competent forehand, a lackluster player can intimidate opponents unprepared for the speed at which the stroke can propel the ball. This proclivity is not restricted merely to players of average skills. Many a professional is less than joyful at the prospect of facing either Marty Hogan or Steve Serot—pros whose forehands travel at speeds over 140 mph.

Primarily an offensive weapon, the forehand is also used to serve, hit overhead strokes and volley off the front wall.

Before you can hope to stroke any of these blows, however, it's necessary to know how to hold the racquet, stand and then swing the forehand stroke.

The first thing to be aware of is there is a specific, correct way to grip the racquet.

It's vital this be mastered, as a slight variation is all that's needed to deliver the backhand.

One quick blurb before getting to the essentials. As the majority of the world's population is composed of right-handed individuals (an area in which the author differs markedly) instruction will be geared to the righties. Indignant left-handers are requested to swallow their pride and substitute left when they come across directions stressing the right hand, arm or other extremity.

Armed with a competent forehand, a player can intimidate opponents unprepared for the speed at which the stroke can propel the ball.

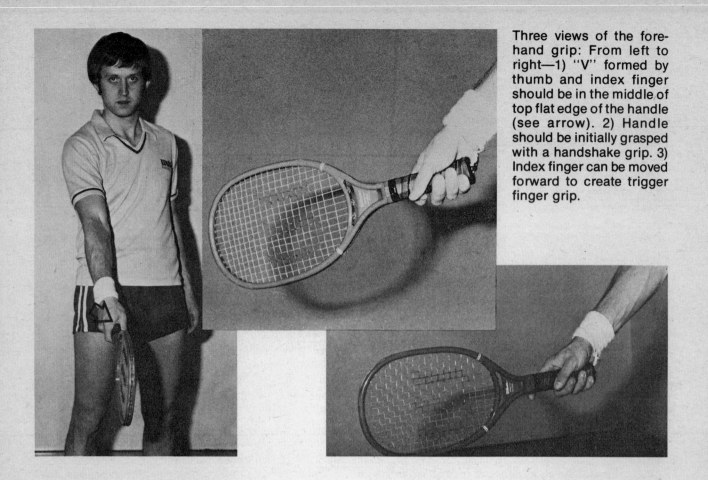

Three views of the forehand grip: From left to right—1) "V" formed by thumb and index finger should be in the middle of top flat edge of the handle (see arrow). 2) Handle should be initially grasped with a handshake grip. 3) Index finger can be moved forward to create trigger finger grip.

The Forehand Grip

The first thing to do when assuming the proper forehand grip is to address your racquet in a friendly fashion.

There's no need to fondle or caress the racquet, just shake hands with it.

Seriously speaking, the best way to approach the grip is hold the racquet aloft with your left hand (right for the sake of the lefties). Place the shooting hand palm flat on the strings and move the palm downward. Continue descent until your palm is wrapped around the handle. Your fingers should be spread slightly, with the "V" formed by the thumb and index finger directly in line with the middle of the flat edge of the handle.

A note of caution here. Once you've established the grip don't feel you have to mold to your fingers permanently in place on the handle.

Don't feel poorly if you don't master the grip the first time around. When practicing, try to compare your grip with the variations that follow, so as to pick out areas that need improvement. (By the way, it's a good idea to practice before a full-length mirror in your spare time.)

Once you've grasped the racquet properly with the handshake grip a few details remain to be considered. First, take your index finger and move it slightly up the handle, about ½-inch to be exact. This maneuver will extend control over the handle and thusly the racquet.

It's worthwhile to become accustomed to the feel of this trigger finger grip. Many a missed shot will prove you can never have too much control.

All of these tips are easily relayed, but somewhat harder to put into practice. So once again, don't feel a bit inept, uncoordinated or out of it if you don't get it all right at first. To prove the point read on, we'll cover some of the more commonly made grip errors.

A major error that often takes place can be called "the curse of the iron grip." The fingers clasp the handle in a manner designed to make a strong hand quake. The fingers are clutched tightly together far down the handle with no separation between the index finger and thumb. Use of such a grip will allow the hitter to punish the ball when he hits it, but control suffers.

Another common flaw is the grip we'll dub the fate of the twisted hand. This happenstance is reminiscent of an individual moving forward quickly to shake an acquaintance's hand. Dominating the encounter, the shaker's hand envelops the partner's with the result of a drastic overlap.

This relationship can be applied to the forehand grip in two fashions, neither desirable.

In the first the handshake overlaps the side of the handle, so the "V" formed is out of sync. As a result the racquet face is not perpendicular to the floor as desired, but slanted downwards. This is called a "closed face."

Contacting the ball with this grip the forehand will unerringly pound it in the direction the racquet points—directly into the floor. This tactic is most unrewarding; the rules remind us the ball must hit the front wall first.

The other variation of the twisted grip takes place when the racquet face is slanted toward the ceiling. With this "open face" in use the hitter will find the majority of his or her strokes rocketing upward. More often than not opponents will leap at the opportunity to cream these floaters.

Moving from the perils of the twisted hand, we go to the territory of the overreaching shake. This transgression is common in social circles when one individual displays great intensity in greeting another. Striding crisply to clasp hands the shaker catches the quarry off guard. As a result the shakee's hand is almost completely overlapped.

Applied to the racquet handle the procedure is almost directly opposite the iron grip. A glance reveals the entire hand, especially the index finger high up on the handle, virtually touching the throat. About the only thing that can be said for this grip is that the forehand poke delivered will be weak at best.

Occasionally a player will come up with a bizarre grip which provides surprisingly good results. The beginner should note the grip, smile at the eccentricity, wish the player well, and return to the fundamentals. Once the proper grip has been conquered, it's time to discuss some pertinent addendums.

The question is often raised, "exactly where should my hand fit on the handle, towards the throat or down by the butt?"

The answer is close to the butt, but just a smidgen above. It's obvious there are a host of positions in which the handle can be grasped. Disregard the example shown in photo 1, which is reminiscent of little grip at all. Do the same with the dismal exercise displayed in photo 2, a sure example of strangulation of the racquet throat. The proper approach is demonstrated in photo 3, where the butt of the racquet rests slightly below the fleshy part of the palm. This grasp will place all fingers in good position on the handle, with ample room for movement and adjustment.

Oh yes, there's one more topic that definitely merits further discussion. Many players, adult males in particular, demonstrate an inclination towards squeezing the handle into a form of putty.

When attempting to formulate the proper grip, there's no need, repeat no need, to permanently encrust the digits around the handle for time immemorial. When meeting the ball the forehand grip should be tightly applied, but not so that a coat of oil is required to free the racquet.

In fact, prior to setting up the grip the fingers should be relaxed around the handle, in a state of easy readiness.

It may take some doing, and no one said it would be easy, but after practice, some more practice and a little more, even the most clumsy-handed should be confident with his forehand grip.

Hand positions: 1) Hand too far back will increase power and reduce control. 2) Too far forward sacrifices speed and control. 3) Proper position with heel of racquet against heel of hand.

The Backhand Grip

That matter disposed of we'll adjourn to the other half of the grip spectrum, the backhand.

Now the backhand is a curious thing. Few of us have had much occasion to use our backhands in baseball, basketball, softball, football and the like. Tennis players are acquainted with the stroke, but they will find some difference between the net game's version and racquetball.

To begin with, many people, the author included find the backhand motion rather deviant in nature. "Now hold on a minute," you may say. "Isn't it true a player can generate more power with a backhand than a forehand? Isn't it because the hitting arm is extended away from the body, while it crosses over the torso in the forehand?"

The only answers that can be offered to these physiological queries, are yes, and yes again. However, despite the fact the backhand may intrinsically be more powerful, the majority of players have more trouble with it than the forehand.

It's only natural in a way. After all, how many times have you pitched a baseball or thrown a spiral from the backhand side.

Pushing the great debate aside, suffice to say it's mandatory for the player to possess the correct grip for the backhand.

Once the forehand grip has been mastered the backhand grip tends to follow quickly. "How come?" you ask. The answer is simple: The backhand grip is identical to the forehand, except for one difference.

That difference, just a twist of the racquet, is often the fine point between success and failure.

The procedure for establishing the backhand grip can be casually stated. Hold the racquet in the proper forehand grip, then rotate the top of the racquet slightly forward of perpendicular (away from the body).

The exact amount of this rotation is a subject of discussion among experts. Some extoll the virtues of a quarter-turn, others an eighth-, others stand fast for the measurement of "slight." The majority of pros seem to land closer to the one-eighth side, and that's as good a choice as any.

A glance quickly reveals the difference between the forehand grip and the backhand. Now the question that may spring to mind is "Why is it so important to twist the racquet this or that much? Wouldn't the same grip work just as well and be a whole lot easier?"

The answers to these questions, which are good ones by the way, are: if you don't turn the racquet your shots will fly upward, and no it wouldn't. Sometimes the old tale of a picture being worth a thousand words is worth employing.

Take another look at the photos on page 22. See how the famous "V" is lined up with the middle of the handle in the forehand grip.

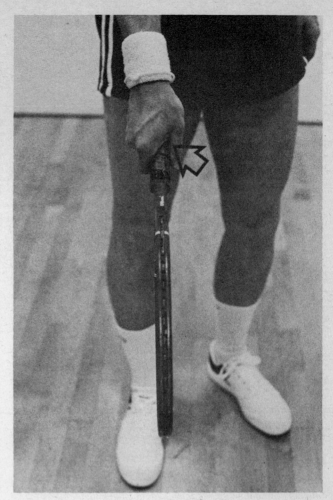

Above and below—The backhand grip. Note that the "V" formed by forefinger and thumb is over the left edge of the handle flat.

Now look at the backhand version. See how the "V" lines up with the left edge of the handle. By making the shift the head of the racquet will be directly in sync with the path you want the ball to follow after contact. This effort is achieved with the forehand without the racquet twist.

Try it a while, and you're sure to say it's really uncomfortable. To tell you the truth, I agree. Unfortunately, the backhand grip has stood the test of play and it's the only way to go. Unless you relish the thought of

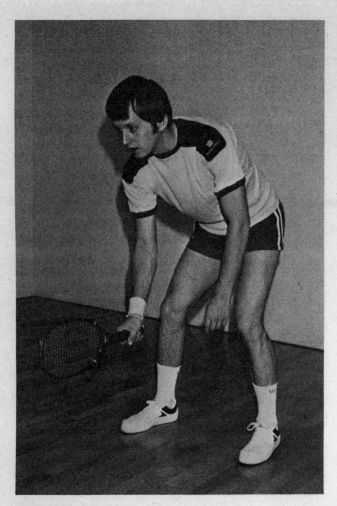

The ready stance—knees slightly bent, head and torso leaning forward, and racquet poised near the right knee.

repetitive defeat, that is.

Practice it for a while, and try to develop a ready feel for it on contact. Once this affinity is developed it's time for the next bit of dogma concerning the grips.

Other than when you're serving the ball it's impossible to know precisely whether your next shot will be a fore- or backhand. Yet it's necessary to alter the grip with each shift in stroke. How do you go about being prepared and ready to shift at the proper time?

Force of habit is the answer, although at this time it may not sound at all reassuring. Take it as a given though; by constantly practicing the shift in grip from forehand to backhand you'll get the hang of it. Of course it won't work too well at first, even in front of a mirror, and the racquet may slip every now and then.

Here's some preventive medicine that can be a bit hard to swallow. In the process of making the switch you may be tempted to use your other hand (the one not holding the racquet) to facilitate the turn. There's nothing wrong with this procedure if you have time to do it. But sometimes the opportunity to dally just isn't

there. Especially when you're near the front wall and the ball comes blurring towards you.

So use that other claw if you have to, but try to remember racquetball is best played as a one-handed game.

The Stance

After familiarity with the grips has been achieved, thoughts of delivering crisp strokes from either side invariably start to kindle. It's a little early to start smoking however. The next step you'll need to master is how to stand as the ball comes your way.

It may appear overstated, but it's vital for a player to be relaxed when the action arrives. As the ball comes hurtling toward you, or dying, in some instances, you must be capable of reacting—quickly.

Believe it or not there's a certain posture which is virtually guaranteed to place your body in a state of optimum readiness. Compared to yoga and other disciplines which require years of study, racquetball's "ready" position is easily achieved. In fact, all it takes to master the technique is the ability to crouch and concentrate.

The first thing to do before you meet the ball is of paramount importance—remain calm. The next is to bend the knees, slightly, head dipping forward and hold the racquet near your right knee. The head of the racquet should be raised slightly toward the left shoulder (lefties read right) so as to aid in the backswing.

While you're awaiting service it's okay to place both hands on the racquet. After all, the ball can't sneak up on you until it's been served.

When you can picture yourself comfortably crouched, ready to dart left or right, you're positioned to move on cue. Before springing forward with your shot however, keep one more thing in mind. Try to keep as much of your weight as possible on your back foot. The added momentum when pushing off will add to the power of the stroke.

You'll quickly realize it doesn't take much practice (and that's one of few times you'll hear that) to master. It's fortunate, as the next step in the process is nowhere as easily grasped.

The next stage requires the fledgling to stride purposefully toward the ball and begin the stroke that will produce a sure winner.

In order to do so, you have to take the ready position one step further, into what's called the setup stage (it may not be the most original phrase, but it's readily comprehensible).

It's important to realize racquetballs are most often stroked from a sideways stance. This means any notion you may have of deftly swatting the ball directly from the ready position should recede into oblivion. The idea is to maximize the power and speed of the shot, something that's very difficult to accomplish from a standstill.

The typical racquetball stroke— ideally it's made from a sideways stance which allows greater control and power.

After hearing the above commentary concerning sideways play, it's likely to raise a few eyebrows. For the benefit of readers unable to cope with the thought there's ground for hope. After stroking the ball the body returns to an easily recognizable forward posture.

Getting back to the setup, the player in the ready position sights the ball and springs into motion.

As the ball comes closer the player should move into a sideways posture with most body weight on the back foot. The racquet should be brought back into the backswing. In case you're wondering how high should the backswing be, take a forehand grip and extend the racquet arm, fully bent, behind and to the right. If you've accomplished this maneuver successfully, the racquet should be in line with your right ear (lefties, remember to switch). Your elbow should be bent almost fully back, forming a near perfect "V" with the forearm. A glance downward will show this "V" virtually in line with the right foot.

By way of clarification a right-hander will turn towards the right sidewall when launching a forehand and the left sidewall prior to a backhand.

The ability to move quickly into the setup position is worth the amount of time required to get it right. It should be practiced on court often and at home, with the aid of a mirror.

Admittedly, it may feel silly, practicing moving from a crouch to a sideways motion. When you get bored, or think how silly it must look, just daydream into the future. Picture yourself moving deftly towards a shot. It may be a bit Mittyesque, but the reverie will make the practice a little easier.

Besides, think of it in this light. What logically follows after you're ready to hit the ball? Why making the shots. And that's what racquetball is all about.

CHAPTER 6

The Forehand

CONTINUING ON in the vein most readers are right-handers we'll examine the forehand stroke.

When discussing the forehand it's helpful to recall there are a number of shots that fit under its umbrella. Let's begin with the most commonly admired, the hard straight drive toward the front wall.

The forehand drive is the big bang in any self-respecting player's arsenal. Held in esteem by competitors and spectators alike, the flashy stroke elicits grudging nods of admiration from opponents, and supportive coos from onlookers. It's the shot most beginners want to master first and show their friends.

There's plenty of reason for the admiration. Every sport possesses a certain action which invariably creates excitement. Baseball has its home run, football the long touchdown pass. Basketballers thrill to a backboard rending duck-shot, while tennis aficionados grin at the sight of a rocketing ace.

Welding together the power of an athlete's legs, torso, shoulder, arms and wrists, the forehand drive is racquetball's thrillmaker. Within its own four-walled arena the stroke is often thought of as the game's grim reaper.

And with good reason. In the hands of top professionals a forehand drive can be a withering experience, traveling wallward at speeds seemingly too fast to follow. Viewed from the gallery the ball resembles a rubbery blur which cracks off the wall with a loud pop.

By no means a finesse shot, the forehand drive can be an exercise in finality. When struck off the lower 6 inches of the front or side walls it is meant to be a rally-ender. More often than not the shot successfully terminates play. Little wonder then that version has been dubbed the "kill."

A fascinating aspect concerning the forehand drive in particular and racquetball in general is that anyone can master the shots. In fact, the most feared shot in the game is actually one of the easiest to produce. The reason for this accessibility is that for most people the forehand stroke comes naturally.

The best way to approach the study of the stroke is to examine its components. As the nearby series of photos reveal, impact occurs as a full-swing (or pendulum-like motion) runs its course. Propelled onward by the full force of the body unwinding the ball has no choice but to carom forward rapidly.

Closeup of forehand stroke demonstrates pendulum-like swing.

Forehand stroke (from left to right): 1) Set position. 2) Full Backswing and weight transfer. 3) Step . . .

It's impossible to seriously study the forehand drive without the following concept being thoroughly and totally understood. What good is it to stroke a terrific shot if you're out of position when you shoot it? The proper place to establish position for the forward drive is about one step away from the point of impact. This logistic can be attained by gauging the path of the ball and staying cautiously behind it. It takes a while, but after that while, you'll learn when to step in and strike the ball. You'll reap the benefit of most always making contact at the proper height off the floor.

That height, upon which so much to follow depends, is one of racquetball's most sternly etched commandments. It reads "knee high or thereabouts" and should never be forsaken. As the idea is to direct the ball forward in as straight a line as possible, a knee high trajectory is the ideal to rally around. If the drive is struck lower it will go forth lower, which is not always advisable. If struck higher it will fly upwards—sometimes the wrong way to go. If the proper stroke is desired, remember the where-to as well as the how-to of hitting it.

So let the probe begin, as the ball comes rocketing forward along the right-hand side of the court.

Sighting the ball in flight the shooter springs into the setup posture. Body weight begins to be transferred to the back foot, as the racquet arm begins the ascent of the backswing. Next, the weight has been firmly shifted

and is ready for acceleration. The racquet arm is fully poised in the backswing, with the wrist cocked and ready to unwind.

The "V" juncture of the forearm and upper arm has been established, with the forearm at about a right angle from the upper arm. At this point in time the shooter is poised and ready to move into and through the ball. Just a note: There is no other stance in racquetball which when visually isolated portrays the player in such a statuesque yet intimidating fashion.

Once the basics have been accomplished, the stroke begins a lightning descent. The most noticeable event to occur is the initiation of the racquet's descent. Perched high atop the backswing the racquet is about to sweep downward toward a show-stopping collision with the ball. As the racquet begins this journey several other equally important motions are taking place.

For starters, note the shift in position of the hips and knees. Whereas seconds ago they were virtually frozen in place they have begun to flow forward. Moving laterally the weight transfer to the front (left) foot has begun.

As the legs surge forward, so does the arm and shoulder. With a smooth motion the shoulder of the racquet arm has begun to lower, aiding the racquet in its vertical descent.

Functioning as a direction finder, this shoulder shift will prompt the racquet arm to follow its prescribed course, and slice toward the ball on a level keel.

. . . forward and racquet arm starting downward arc. 4) Follow-through with low bend.

As the racquet arm proceeds in its sweeping arc downward, the hips and knees continue their forward bending extensively. Firmly in control they allow the player to step forward, and initiate the surge of momentum.

As this step forward is undertaken the body's stance begins to differ markedly. Whereas moments ago the player's frame was relatively compact, coiled for action, the unit has now begun to unwind.

While the preparatory posture was mostly vertical, the stroke itself forces the body to flow horizontally. In order to cope with this change in thrust, the frame reacts to maintain its sense of balance. The non-shooting hand and arm emerge as a balancing pole in a tightrope act, moving away from the body. The elbow of the shooting hand is tucked close to the body.

Once a stable position has been secured (body stepping forward, racquet arm moving down and other arm counterbalancing) the stroke moves toward impact. The racquet arm continues its sweeping, downward arc with the elbow serving as guide. The forearm is parallel to the floor, fully bent at the elbow. With the wrist still firmly cocked the racquet is quickly building up a full head of steam.

At this moment the ball is fast approaching and the racquet advances to offer greetings. Just prior to impact the racquet shoulder has swung down and points to the floor. At this time the elbow begins to unbend and the racquet face is perpendicular to the floor. As the ball steams in at roughly knee-high level, the collision takes place in the span between mid-torso and the front foot.

The racquet, horizontal to the floor on contact, continues forward after the blow has been struck. The majority of the body's weight has shifted to the front foot while the player continues eye contact at the point of impact.

This shift is of vital importance, as it provides another linkup in the delivery system. While the racquet arm surged forward buoyed by the momentum of the weight shift it still required a set point at which to strike. This reference base took the form of the front foot, which bore the brunt of the pendulum-like motion. With one foot firmly planted on substantive ground, the floorboards, the racquet arm was free to unleash all the speed it developed enroute.

More than simply striking out at the ball with the racquet face, however, the wrist cock also delivers its due. No early bloomer, the cocked wrist reserved the best for last, unwinding a mini-second before contact. The wrist snap serves a key function for without it the forehand drive would be sapped of much of its power. Dealing the ball a firm hit the wrist snap continues on past contact. This post-impact phase provides a measure of power which adds that extra zing to the shot. Try to think of it as an after-shock, and the force becomes clearer.

Forehand stroke sequence (counter-clockwise from top right) demonstrates: 1) Set position. 2) Weight transfer and step forward. 3) Impact point with racquet parallel to floor. 4) Body weight on front foot and smooth follow-through to termination.

Note the position of the racquet arm as it delivers the wrist snap and enters the next stage. All components involved in contact (arm, wrist and racquet) have merged into a straight line. While this aids in guiding the path of the ball toward the target, its motion serves another end.

After generating the force of impact the forehand stroke must run through to conclusion, or else jerk abruptly to a halt. An abrupt halt would result in both a poorly stroked shot and a bruised set of back muscles. So the forehand drive continues on toward termination (follow-through) to help alleviate undue strain. The legs bend forward to release some of the pressure they have withstood throughout. Maintaining the horizontal striking posture the frame continues to bend low so as to encounter the least resistance.

Terminating the powerful arc that kindled so much thrust, the racquet arm moves toward the left side of the body. It slows up only when it has run out of gas (about a foot or so past the torso).

Practice

The problem with any instructional device, prose or picture, is that it often promises to lead the reader to the promised land but fails to deliver. Granted, the best of words cannot be translated into action, but they should serve to lay out the route to travel.

It's true that any marginally coordinated player can develop a lethal forehand; in case you've begun to question your potential. But only if the fundamentals are mastered, and that takes a lot of doing. Doing by the way, is spelled P-R-A-C-T-I-C-E.

One encouraging note, though; once you begin to put together the pieces, practice can become enjoyable. What could be boring about doing your best to belt, swat, or flail a ball toward the front wall? With time your efforts may become slightly more refined, but initial attempts are always exciting at least.

Despite the fun of those introductory wild and wooly strokes, too much of a fun thing can eventually become boring.

Unfortunately, boredom generally occurs just when you've got the backswing, wrist cock and weight transfer in gear.

In order to create a more perfect and less boring practice session, there are several strategies you can employ.

First, try to have fun with the forehand drive. Once you feel the rudiments are in place, use some creativity in refining them.

Try hitting the ball from waist height, for a while; then practice stroking it from a carom off the front wall. When you think you've got the hang of it, move to different positions on the court and repeat. You can never practice too much. Hit the drive by bouncing the ball in front of you and stepping into the shot. Continually try to improve your ability to gauge the position,

Downward shift of racquet arm shoulder along with forward bend of hips and knees help player initiate surge of momentum.

Cocked wrist starts to unwind almost at point of impact. The wrist snap adds considerable power to the forehand stroke.

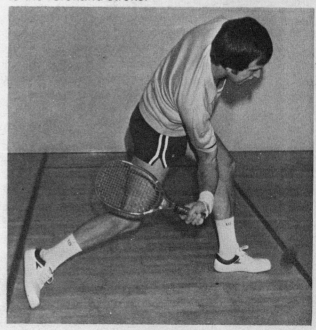

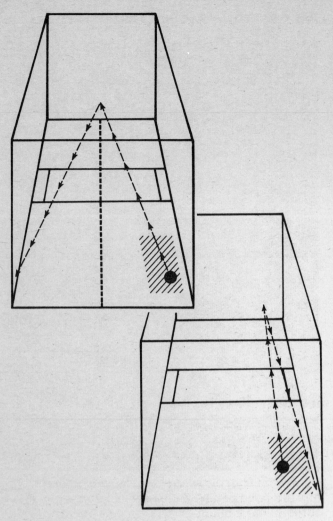

Forehand cross-court (upper) and down-the-line (lower) drives diagramed. Dotted line in the cross-court represents midpoint of court's width.

direction and flight speed of the ball.

Mastery of the forehand drive entitles the bearer to more than the right to mercilessly pound the ball off the walls. Used correctly, and deviously, the shot can be wielded in several effective fashions. Although they'll be discussed in depth later, here's a taste of some of the goodies.

The Down-the-Line

One such application is known as the down-the-line ball. The terminology may seem bizarre, but it's thoroughly descriptive. The down-the-line shot is performed exactly as stated. On those occasions when the shooter is stationed near a side wall he or she may wish to catch the opponent off-guard with a winner. If the foe is stationed at center court or slightly to the other side, the moment is right. Following through on the fundamentals the shooter will direct the ball straight forward, on a line paralleling the side wall. Hit properly the shot will either be low enough to serve as a kill, or function as a passing shot. (More on that later.)

The Cross-Court Drive

On other occasions the shooter may be positioned slightly to one side of center court as the ball steams closer. When the opponent is situated in center court, near the front wall (within 10 to 15 feet) the circumstance calls for a crosscourt drive.

Vigorously stroking the drive off front wall center, the ball will rebound and move past the left hand side of the opponent for a winner.

There are two trajectories with which this shot can be best directed. Each describes a "V" flight path from the hitter to the front wall and back past the opposition. Properly struck each shot will expire near the rear corner to which it's headed.

Unfortunately it's not yet the proper time to delve into the machinations of these strokes. Have patience though. After we digest the main meal of fundamentals, dessert will be a real treat.

The Kill

Dessert, in racquetball parlance, is spelled K-I-L-L, the name of the most final shot in the game.

There's nothing quite like the kill shot in any other sport. It's a stroke both savage and beautiful, delivered on offense and defense. Speeding wallward no more than 6 inches off the floor the stroke is meant to curtail a rally abruptly, bouncing twice before the opponent can retrieve it.

For players and spectators alike it is the glamor shot; the stroke that sends shivers through opponents.

While it undoubtedly serves as an asset oncourt, the kill shot also functions as one of the game's greatest promotional aids.

More than a few non-players have been drawn towards the court after watching a perfect kill come off the wall. Unlike sports wherein only the most talented hit the home runs or score touchdowns, the kill is within the grasp of most players.

"After all," it's easily reasoned, "if I can hit the ball off the wall, why shouldn't I be able to hit it low?"

With the dream of glory kindled, many newcomers have come forth to pursue their quest. For the majority, a successful kill will soon be theirs in the future. All it takes is the time spent in practicing the fundamentals.

In fact, from the moment the forehand drive is mastered the player can begin thinking of that first competition kill.

It's easy to picture a slew of readers saying out loud "I don't believe it. Why look at all that's involved with just the forehand stroke. Between learning the components and trying to get the form right I'm up to my ears in confusion. Suddenly you're going to tell us something can come easy. That's a trap if I ever heard one."

Before you hurl the text in disgust, relax for a second. If you can stroke a reasonable facsimile of a forehand you will be able to hit an effective kill shot.

CHAPTER 7

The Backhand

Unlike tennis, the racquetball player cannot "run around the backhand." An attempt to shoot from pictured position will result in damaged racquet.

WITH A PROMISE that the secrets of the kill and other strokes mentioned will come your way in the near future, let's tackle the backhand.

It may seem unfair to dangle the sweets and retract them but there's just no fair way to induce concentration upon the backhand. It's something many a newcomer would rather live without. In fact, the majority of newcomers and quite a few veterans share a common mistrust of all shots from the backhand side.

What's amusing about this mean-spirited view is once a player develops a backhand drive he or she becomes most eager to flaunt it.

The sad part of the tale though is the flipside. Without practice the backhand can most definitely be titled the novice's bane.

This label is more often found on the tennis court where it's labeled "running around the backhand." The problem with doing the same within the racquetball court are the dimensions. It's well-nigh impossible to run around a crisp forehand drive as the walls leave little room for maneuvering in the corners. Pinning the body tightly into the left corner (lefties read right) the shooter presses the flesh against the sidewall. Scrunching up the shoulder, the racquet arm raises vertically, and makes an awkward swipe at the ball. The majority of these sweeps are fruitless, those that succeed are only slightly less so.

There's no need for a newcomer to experience such embarrassment, however. Initial and persistent rehashing of the fundamentals to follow will hopefully unlock the door to the backhand. With the stroke firmly in hand, accompanied by the forehand drive, the player will have the tools for success.

The first thing to note in eyeing the backhand is what not to do. Remember the grip is not the same as with the forehand. Failure to switch grips on each backhand effort is the fastest step to frustration available. So remember, switch grips on the backhand.

Although the backhand is disliked for a wealth of reasons, most failing efforts suffer from a few fatal flaws. Whereas with the forehand most everyone manages to take a wholehearted, all-out swipe at the ball, few do the same with the backhand.

2—Moving forward, weight begins to transfer to front foot. The backswing begins the descent.

3—Continuing diagonal step forward, racquet arm moves lower and begins to extend.

1—Backhand begins with proper stance, backswing in place, weight back on the left foot.

6—Shoulder and racquet arm continue to pull through after contact; wrist snap is complete and the body is engaged in follow-through.

7—Bent to waist level, the shooting arm and shoulder flow with the motion.

4—Just prior to impact body is ready to uncoil. The wrist is about to snap, adding another dash of force to the blow.

9—(Below) Winding through to resolution, the racquet arm is virtually vertical.

8—The torso continues onward with the racquet arm beginning its upward flow.

Closeup picture series demonstrates correct way to setup and approach the backhand drive.

On many occasions the sight of novice backhands borders on the pitiful. Full-bodied men and women stand crouched in the ready position awaiting the ball. Moving towards contact the racquet begins its forward motion, aided by the body's momentum. Opponents and onlookers alike ready their ears for a boisterous pop when strings meet rubber. What they get is a barely audible tick. Instead of racquet, arm and player functioning as one smoothly running unit, the components became disassembled during the swing. Instead of moving towards the ball the shooter has lost the ability to extend the torso forward. While the ball should normally be greeted by the racquet, the racquet stands idle by the player's left-hand side. As the ball sweeps past, the racquet makes an ineffectual, semi-vertical waffle at the sphere. With luck the ball floats high and slowly towards the front wall; a sure loser. Most times, the ball drifts a few feet forward before hitting the floor.

Putting the saga of the flailing backhand follies behind, let's look at the correct way to approach and stroke the puzzler.

Immediately after sighting the backhand-to-be, the player should step sideways to the path of the ball. Having done so, the weight should, like in the forehand, rest primarily on the back foot. The racquet should be brought back as far as possible into the backswing, with the wrist cock being initiated. Once again the body is in a largely vertical position, with the knees bent into a slight crouch. As the ball approaches, the shoulders should begin to move backward so that the shooting shoulder actually faces the backwall. In case you think that's impossible strike the pose in a mirror. Notice the position?

The next stage is imperative as you step diagonally towards the ball, initiating the weight transfer from the back to front leg. At the same time the shooting shoulder and hips begin to glide into the motion.

The racquet arm, up high, still bent, begins to extend.

But, and a big one it is, the racquet remains back, along with the cocked wrist, pending further action.

Now the plot begins to thicken. With the weight transfer virtually completed, the racquet arm nears full extension prior to impact. The racquet arm is held in almost a vertical posture as the shooting shoulder provides a pulling action towards the ball. At this time the wrist snap has begun to break.

At the moment of the merging of ball and racquet, contact is delivered off the front foot. The racquet arm is fully extended, and the wrist has snapped. No, the shot is not quite finished yet. Notice the position of the wrist after contact. Instead of loosening and beginning to fly upward, it remains firm after the snap. The legs have bent under the forward release of power, and the shoulders are no longer tightly coiled. This ability to bend while keeping the racquet face vertical though a firm wrist snap is essential. By greeting the ball in this

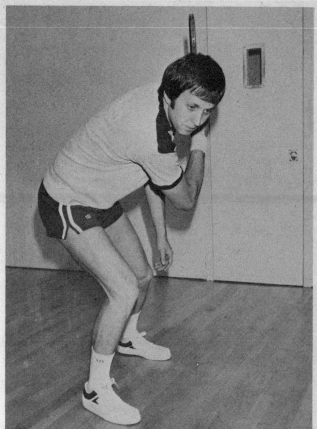

fashion the shot will carry straight ahead. Had the racquet face been either closed or open on contact the ball would respond accordingly: rocketing into the floor or flying too high off the front wall.

The firmly held wrist does more than act as a direction finder. Relaying tremendous power as it unfolds the snap adds a hefty dash of gusto to the shot. Properly executed it will turn a speeding ball into a veritable screamer.

Pay sharp attention to the follow-through. Like the forehand drive where the racquet arm proceeds upward the backhand features a horizontal motion that sweeps high.

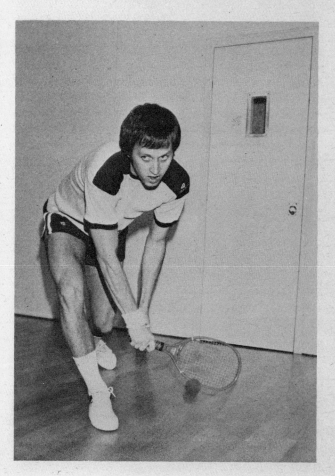

Pulling through after contact the shooting arm and shoulder remain at waist level momentarily, then rise to face the right hand wall. The body remains bent after impact, seeking to maximize the power of the stroke and aid in the retention of balance.

One other point worth noting. While winding and unwinding its way through the forehand drive the non-shooting arm functions as a balance pole. Not so in the backhand, where the arm is held closer to the body. The other arm plays a minimizing role in the stroke, basically trying to avoid impeding the fluidity of the swing.

Judged on the merits of its parts as opposed to the myths surrounding its use, the backhand drive becomes less fearsome. Objectively viewed, even a timorous

As with forehand, the backhand stroke calls for cocked wrist and wrist snap to develop power.

newcomer might admit the development of the shot is well within his or her potential. Take it from hordes of players who have overcome backhand backlash to make the most of their potential. All that's required is more of that tiresome dirge, practice.

Practice

Utilizing the drills designed to strengthen the forehand drive, apply the same to the backhand. Try to put in more time on the backhand however. It's well known whatever comes hardest is often first ceased, especially in the rehearsal stage.

Like the forehand, the backhand drive can be used to streamline shots down the line, or send the ball crosscourt. Backhand kills are a much rarer entity than their opposite number, but a worthwhile weapon to possess. Keep it in mind when you go out to practice, then run through the routine again.

When it comes to that routine, don't feel penned in by a specific regimen. While it's necessary to begin by stationing yourself in a set position (perhaps 10 feet past the short line) with time you'll be able to innovate.

Practice stroking self-bounced backhands at 5-foot intervals from the service line. When you've retreated as far as the backwall, switch sides and move forward.

Then start again, only hit the stroke off caroms from the front wall.

Alternate crosscourt shots with down-the-line shots until you feel comfortable with each.

Whenever you feel a wave of boredom about to ooze forth, stop for a moment.

Take a deep breath and picture your friends' surprise when they see your backhand drive.

Suddenly, it can seem worthwhile to hit just a few more.

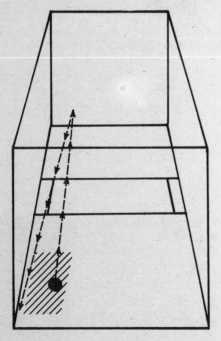

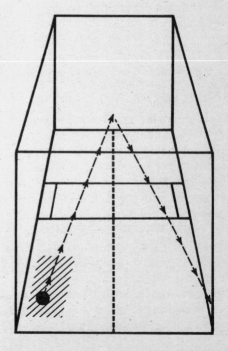

Down-the-line pass (left) and cross-court drive (right) shots from the backhand. Dotted line in cross-court diagram represents center of court.

CHAPTER 8

Some Problems

REGARDLESS OF YOUR diligence there are going to be moments when the strokes don't go your way. Sometimes the forehand will betray you, another day the backhand will go astray.

There's no need to flail the air (or wall) with your racquet in despair. Nor is it necessary to call in a courtside Sherlock Holmes to solve the mystery of the inconsistent stroke. All that's required is a healthy dose of self-examination.

Let's examine the forehand. The initial opportunity for disaster can occur prior to the shot. Look in a mirror or ask a friend or competitor if you're in the proper setup position before the ball arrives. Failure to be prepared can cause several dubious outcomes: A tardy approach will cause you to make contact too late, depriving the shot of power and direction. An over-anxious attack can have equally disastrous consequences. The key to success is the efficient unwinding of a body coiled for action. If you find your setup behind schedule, follow each shot more closely, and act accordingly. If over-anxiousness is the problem, hold the swing in check until the ball is almost upon you.

Another possible problem area is the grip. It's one thing to have a perfect grip before the ball is in play, another to maintain it throughout the stroke. With the need to shift the grip from fore- to backhand it's easy to forget or to make an incorrect adjustment. All it takes is a slight miscalculation to prompt an horrendous stroke.

Keep in mind the "V" juncture of the thumb and index finger should rest on the middle of the topmost flat of the handle in the forehand grip.

Weight transfer is another critical area. When delivering either stroke body weight should be smoothly transfered from the back to front foot. The process allows the ball to be struck with the maximum in bodily momentum. If your weight remains on the back foot after impact it's a sure sign of trouble. If you failed to step forward the prospect is also bleak. The only answer to these problems is to practice the fundamentals, preferably with a sharp partner.

Many individuals are victimized by problems concerning placement of the non-shooting arm during the forehand. The appendage in question is often contorted

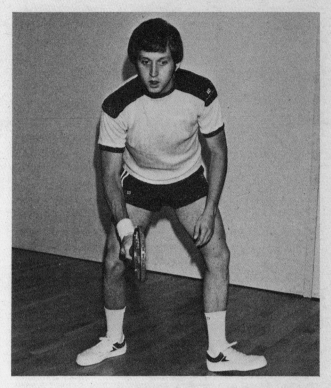

Above—Failure to setup for a shot in time deprives the shot of power and direction.

Below—Iron grip on racquet handle will allow power, but control of the ball suffers.

Above—Non-shooting hand on racquet prevents efficient backhand grip.

Right—Failure to rotate racquet for backhand grip will result in misdirected shot—here toward ceiling.

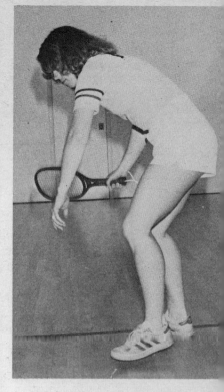

Non-hitting hand can interfere with shot—here preventing proper shoulder rotation.

into bizarre positions. A most costly error occurs when the arm is pinned to the trunk rather than extended outward like a balancing pole; the arm hugs the body, impending a smooth delivery. As a result the shot lacks speed and is ineffective. Overcome the problem with self-discipline and practice.

Some players are possessed of a fear of high speeds, the kind that arise when a rubber rocket draws near. Reactions to high velocity shots to the forehand side can be both comically and visually painful.

Unwilling to totally surrender, the player moves aside, stands rigid with knees straight, and extends the racquet toward the ball. Suffice to say the nearly swing-less motion barely dents the sphere on impact. Perhaps all-out capitulation would have been a wiser choice. Solution: have a friend hit some hard drives in your direction. Eventually you'll master the fear.

Another mishap is the absence of a full and hearty follow-through. This happens when a beginner becomes so excited to have made contact he or she halts the racquet arm immediately after impact. The shot may still reach the front wall, but the beauty pause has minimized its power. Caution: don't admire a shot until it has produced a winner.

Other newcomers may find themselves insecure prior to launching a backhand stroke. As such they commit the sin we'll dub "the hand that came for dinner." The title refers to the overlong tenure of the non-shooting hand upon the racquet face. Remaining affixed until the backswing has started, the unwelcome guest prevents an efficient grip. The ensuing stroke will be ill-conceived at best. Take heed: if the "other" hand must visit make sure the stay doesn't overstay the ready position.

One other point concerns eyesight: The earlier you arrive at a set position before stroking, the better. Naturally your arrival time is dependent upon how early the ball was sighted. Rapid visual pickup will enable you to move with greater decisiveness and eliminate errors. There's only one way to sharpen your vision, though. Play often and keep the eyes open at all times.

Odds are, the majority of readers will experience the greatest difficulty with the backhand drive. Luckily, most players possess failings that are easily corrected. The most common error features the grip. Don't forget it differs from the forehand, and that twist of the racquet makes all the difference.

It would seem an eighth of a turn of the racquet wouldn't make that much difference, but without it you're shooting wild. The slight rotation enables the racquet face to be vertically parallel to the front wall at the point of impact. A change in position, favoring either floor or ceiling will result in the ball acting accordingly. Concentrate on changing grips in practice and

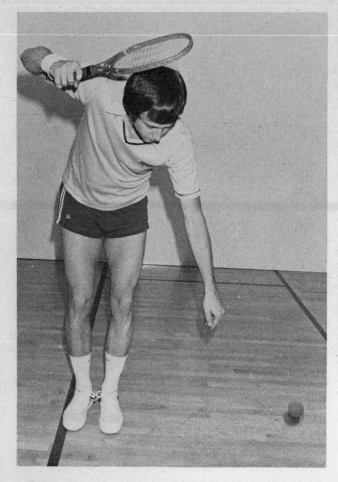

Above—"The stigma of the shy hitter." Failure to lineup sideways will give late backhand.

Left—Bent knees and hips are necessary for proper leverage—delayed hit will result here.

during play. Give it enough time and you'll come to make the switch naturally.

"Does your brain know where your other (non-hitting) hand is during the shot," is a question a troubled backhander might pose. Far too often the non-hitting hand is clutched to the body as the shot begins. This entangling alliance prevents the shooter from fully extending the backswing. It also serves to cripple the stroke, and inhibit shoulder rotation. As with the forehand, practice should solve the problem.

"To crouch, how far to crouch, or not to crouch," is another issue plaguing beginning backhanders. As revealed earlier, bending of the hips and knees is necessary for proper leverage. Sometimes the shooter is overwhelmed with a case of knee bending zealotry. The result is an extremely intimidating, bowled back posture, with racquet held high. Despite the fearsome countenance, the stroke is woeful at best. Another segment of the playing public frowns at the thought of bent knees in its entirety. Befitting such an attitude, the shooter strides somewhat rigormortically into the shot. By way of a refresher, knees and hips should be bent slightly, so as to aid torso rotation and the development of momentum.

Moving on through the list of ailments we come to the dilemma of the flaccid wrist. A crisp wrist snap is the secret of a whistling backhand. By cracking the wrist a

shooter can rely on being able to constantly punish the ball. Unfortunately, it takes training to become accustomed to holding the wrist in a set position. At times the player will fail to cock the wrist properly, with a weak backhand drive forthcoming. There's only one way to overcome the frailty. Fortunately it's as easily done as said. You guessed it—practice. Each time you're on-court solo, check your wrist cock prior to stroking a backhand. Do the same during competition, and ask a friend or observer to keep tabs. If no friends or spectators are available, ask your opponent after the match. By no means question a foe beforehand—not only will he or she claim your form is faultless, they'll exploit it with all due speed. It's worth noting the ease with which the wrist cock can be practiced off court. Just watch your wrist the next time you throw a frisbee.

There are still more uncharted backhand ills to explore: The most treacherous hazard remaining can be titled "the stigma of the shy hitter." Instead of lining up behind and sideways to the ball, many players are caught flatfooted. When this occurs they find the ball has crept up on them, and no time remains to step into the shot. A sickly swipe at the ball takes place featuring poor weight transfer, inadequate arm extension and minimal wrist snap. Nonetheless this stroke is one of the sport's standouts; it's rare to see so many errors incorporated into a single swing.

CHAPTER 9

The Kill Shot

HAVING ENDURED discussion of the errors you're likely to encounter, let's move on to a more pleasurable topic. It's time to savor the dessert—the secrets of the kill shot.

Let's begin with a review of the essentials. The most noticeable aspect is the low height at which the kill travels. This facet is shared by all varieties of the stroke, either fore- or backhand. It can safely be said in lowness lies points. Secondly the kill can be delivered from all positions on the floor, but some are more favorable than others. Third, and this is a biggie, there are several ways in which the blow can be struck off the front wall. These are: the straight kill (the ball bounces directly off the front wall), the side-to-front wall kill, the front-to-side-wall kill and the off-the-back-wall kill.

Newcomers contemplating a kill should remember the shot is a two-edged sword. Just as a well-hit kill will terminate the opposition, a poor stroke can be suicidal.

The only difference between the forehand drive and kill is the height at which the ball is contacted with the racquet. To properly shoot a kill it follows the ball will be struck lower than a regular drive. Consider the area of impact to be from mid-calf to ankle. Naturally the lower the point of contact, the lower the blow will strike the wall. Shots striking 6 inches or lower off the front wall are ideal. In directing the shot the hitter should strive to keep the racquet face level to the path of the ball. Moments when the face is turned floorward (hopefully infrequent) can prove embarrassing to the shooter. Unless, of course, you're able to refrain from blushing when the ball strikes the floor roughly 3 inches after contact.

Once these fundamentals have been etched into the thinktank, practice some kills. There's no need to frown at the thought. It would take a hard-hearted court Scrooge to grimace at the notion of belting the ball low towards the front wall. By the way, if you're wondering just how hard a swing should be unleashed, here's the answer. Never, repeat never swing with all your might. And that goes for any shot in the game.

To a large extent the racquet acts like a catapult, whipping the ball forward. Take advantage of this propulsion factor and swing with a bit less than all your power. You'll still be able to punish the ball while retaining the all-important control needed for accurate placement.

The kill shot should strike the front wall 6 inches or lower from the floor and rebound at an equally low altitude.

Impact area for kill shot should be between calf and ankle.

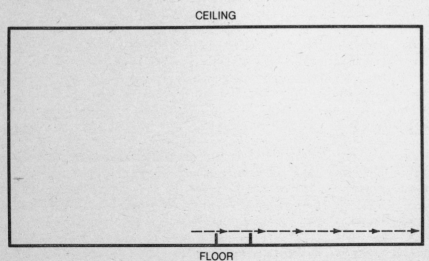

CEILING

FLOOR

Above, left and right—The lower the point of contact with the ball, the lower the blow will strike the front wall. Racquet face must be kept level to the path of the ball.

The kill shot—along with most other shots—should never be hit with full power.

The guidance of the kill is without a doubt its most important component. As with shot making in general the direction finding capability lies in the cerebrum of the shooter.

We mentioned there are several versions of the kill shot. Befitting the strategic aspect of racquetball each is reserved for a specific usage. The primary guide to observe before dishing one up is to think about position, both yours and the opposition. We'll discuss this later in conjunction with overall strategy, but the following shouldn't prove too confusing.

To begin, remember the scoring structure of racquetball. Points can be won only while serving, but are lost each time a return of service is botched. There's no surer way for a kill-happy newcomer to have his ego quashed than a series of futile kills. Basically speaking, the greater the distance from the front wall the greater the difficulty of the kill shot.

It doesn't require an Einstein to judge that when and where to stroke the kill are crucial issues. Ideally speaking the shooter prospers most when the opponent is out of position. For example if your foe is positioned several steps to the left of center court, just behind the service line, the time is ripe for a kill. Assuming the shooter is stationed slightly behind and to the center of the court he or she enjoys a decided advantage. The question which must be resolved rapidly however, is

Front wall-side wall kill shot is used to direct the ball at an oblique angle away from the opponent's position.

which kill to shoot. The alternatives in this case are the straight wall and front sidewall (also known as a pinch shot). Since the opposition is stationed to the left of center, the straight wall kill, hit far to the right is a fine choice. If the stroke is delivered properly the ball should glance off the front wall, and bounce twice before an opponent can reach it. In the case it's improperly delivered, all is still not lost. Many times a kill shot is stroked too high off the floor (calf height and above) or the racquet face is open. When these mishaps occur the kill often becomes an effective drive shot which can speed by your opponent. (These shots called "passing shots" are another of the game's fine points.) This particular pass would be labeled a "down-the-line-ball." There'll be more on the pass later.

So, the straight wall kill can function on its own merits or in a fail-safe capacity.

What, however, if your opponent's off to one side but you still feel he or she can make a return of a straightwall kill? There are times, especially in the early going when what seems like a perfectly good kill comes to no good. Despite the fact the ball was stroked as desired, the opposition was able to make the return on the first bounce. There are two causes for this unfortunate happenstance, both of which will most certainly plague the beginner. Sometimes the hitter will shoot a

kill, but directly in the path of the opponent. Noting the shot a competent player will step forward and greet the ball on the first bounce as if it were a plum ripe for picking. (Just a brief word here on the topic of plums. Any time a shot is hit so poorly it invokes an easy return, it's considered a "plum" in racquetball jargon. So the next time you come across the term disregard the thought of flying fruits whizzing across-court or squashing sickeningly into walls.)

The other probable cause for a self-destructive kill is form. On certain occasions the ball will fly off the wall and bounce high toward mid-court. Instantly the thought races through the shooter's brain cells "This is a perfect time for my new kill shot." Rearing the racquet arm overhead contact is made and the ball heads downward towards the front wall. Striking the wall at a 45-degree angle the ball holds true to the laws of physics—it immediately bounces off the wall downward toward the floor, strikes the floor and bounces upward, another plum to be picked.

Although the newcomer may not have realized it, he has unwittingly unleashed another shot from his utility belt: the overhead drive. While it can function effectively in certain instances it carries a difficulty factor of the highest order. It should be approached with some caution, at least until its mysteries and best uses can be unraveled a few pages hence.

Let's return to the plight of the hitter uncertain about smiting a straight wall kill. When seized with doubt, a front-to-side-wall kill may be the answer. The blow is delivered à la the basic fundamentals of the straight kill shot but with a different destination in mind.

Whereas the straight kill shot wounds by bouncing twice or whizzing by before it can be returned, the front-to-side kill inflicts an angular dose of pain. Ideally speaking the shooter strokes the ball low toward the front wall, but within a 2-foot distance of the far corner. Glancing off the front wall the orb collides with the sidewall, bouncing onto the floor at an oblique angle. The path of the ball should be well beyond the returner's range.

Another variation of the dual-wall kill is the side-front mode, which will also help keep the ball away from the opposition.

A word of caution to all would-be killers reading this text: Both variations of the sidewall kill offer more chance of error than the straight wall effort. The shot must be struck accurately with sufficient force or disaster will ensue—a plumlike rebound to midcourt is a likely offshoot. It's also easy to confuse the target area when aiming at the vicinity of the corner and misfire entirely.

Taking all these facets into consideration decide what's safest for you. Chances are you'll agree and devote the bulk of your kill practice and play to straight wall attempts. At least in the early stages of your career.

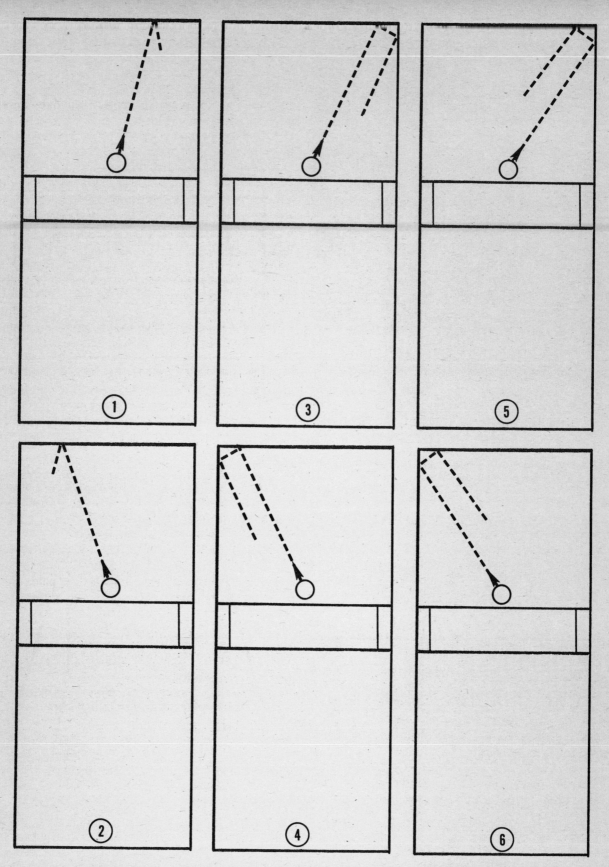

Three ways to kill: 1&2) The straight kill which bounces directly off the front wall. 3&4) The front wall-side wall shot which strikes front wall first and glances off of side wall. 5&6) The side wall-front wall which strikes side wall first before glancing off the front wall.

Side wall-front wall kill must be struck accurately—possibility of error is high.

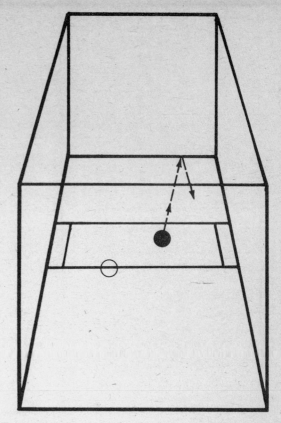

Above and below—Tactical uses of straight and side wall-front wall kills diagrammed. Straight kill (above) is placed to right to keep ball away from opponent situated behind and to left. Side wall-front wall shot can be used when opponent is to right and in front of shooter.

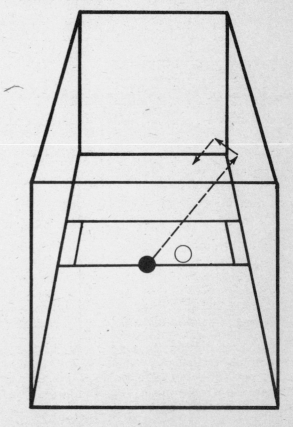

Here's a helpful tip for all would-be court assassins: The closer you are to the front wall when striking the kill, the better (within reason of course). It's difficult to picture a more ghastly prospect than a player standing a foot or so from the wall waiting to hit a kill. Not only will the opponent's shot be too hot to handle, but the thought of returning any more such bullets will foster a case of paranoia.

If you're looking for a general guideline, as to kill or not to kill, try this: *Kill when you're in center court.* After reading this it's only reasonable for readers to wonder exactly where in the center court they should stand. In order to place yourself in the best perch, locate the service box. Step back about 5 feet from the short line and an equal distance from either side wall. This location is cherished territory as it affords maximum opportunities for varying returns and attack.

Throughout this analysis of the kill shot it's bound to be noticed the back-wall kill has been slighted. There's a good reason at this stage of the game. Back wall play is an art of its own, differing considerably from playing the ball directly off a bounce. It's necessary to conquer for success however, so hold your breath and we'll tackle the problem shortly.

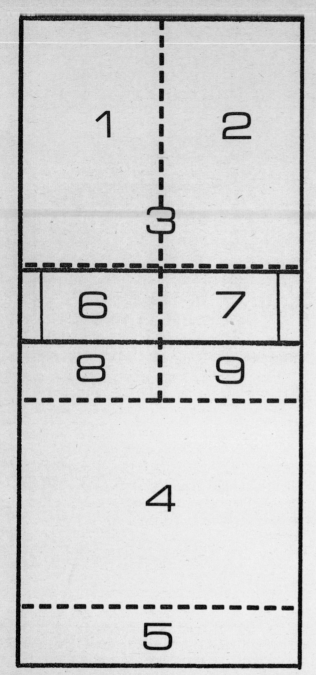

A general guideline: Kill when you're shooting from center court.

The basic hitting areas: When located in zones 1 and 2 feel free to try kills to the left and right corners. The same goes for volleys and dump shots. When located in zone 3 use your discretion as to where to place the shot. Base your decision on your opponent's position. When located in zone 4 refrain from using kill shots unless your opponent is blatantly off to one side or the other. When in zone 5 don't even consider a kill shot unless there's no chance the opponent can make the return. When in zones 6 and 7 make use of left and right corner kills, but be sure to stroke them with precision. You're far away enough to have the shot bounce into midcourt if hit incorrectly. When in zones 8 and 9 use the kill when a perfect opportunity presents itself. You're just a bit removed from maximum effectiveness when shooting from these spots.

Lovers of the backhand can be heard screaming, "What about the backhand kill?". Let's begin by stating many top-ranked amateurs and pros would rather play with a shoe than face life without the backhand kill. In the hands of an experienced player the shot is a necessary part of the court armament.

However, that doesn't imply newcomers should race to unleash the stroke. Whereas most individuals adapt more readily to the forehand than backhand, the same can be said of the backhand drive and kill. While off-target forehand drives can hit high off the front wall and still function as passes, misdirected kills take the opposite route. Backhand kills fired too low are most always terminal.

Many kill shots are carefully planned. A player sees the ball speeding toward the racquet, notes the position, and opts for the kill. If the hitter is positioned properly, there's at least an equal chance the ball will fly towards the forehand side. If the ball is hit deep enough there will be ample time to shift position for a forehand try.

Unless you're one of a distinct minority that favors the backhand this preference will lead to a marked differential in favor of forehand kill attempts.

In addition to being slighted by choice, most players' backhand kill shots lack the conviction of their

Left—Practice the kill shot from varying distances starting at about 10 feet from front wall and gradually increasing. Above—Tape strips forming a box 2 feet by 2 feet aid in practicing pinch shots.

forehand brothers. And if there's one thing a kill cannot be, it's slow-moving. Players stroking crawling kill shots could be accused of acting in the opponent's behalf.

That's not to say the backhand kill should be ignored by beginners. During those first practice sessions as much time should be devoted to the backhand kill as the forehand. Only when the player feels comfortable with the shot, however, should it be incorporated into the weapons bag.

Practice

A while ago you read it can be fun to practice kill shots. For the best results, and a goodly sense of satisfaction try out this routine. Assume the proper ready position (forehand first). Start off about 10 feet from front wall center. Bounce the ball and hit a shot low off the front wall and to the side. Stroke a side-wall kill or two. By starting off close to the front wall even the meekest hitter will be able to crack a kill. Try a few more strokes from this locale, then move back 5 feet at a time. Hit series of five or ten shots at each position. Continue until you're about 5 feet from the back wall. Then do the same from both sides of the court.

Once you feel comfortable with the stroke, return to the first point. Repeat the drill, but with a difference. Hit the kills off balls caroming off the wall (you can throw them if you like). Then go through the entire sequence from the backhand.

Don't forget good defense is an integral part of a heady game, so plan your practice with this view in mind. While long kills from 35 feet may be fun, don't dwell on them. Become proficient from 10 to 25 feet out.

Of course there's always going to be a segment of the population (the author included) which loves a challenge. Rather than have those individuals spend the lion's share of their practice session working on full-court kills, here's a test. Take some tape and walk to the front wall. Place a strip about 2 feet long at the same height from the corner. Extend another strip down to form a box. Then form another box on the adjoining sidewall. Use these boxes as targets for pinch shots throughout your drills. Be sure to shoot series at each from the far backcourt. Unless you can consistently put at least three of five into the box with good velocity, consider the challenge lost. As time goes on by however, your score will improve. The day will arrive when those deep court pinches and kills pepper the boxes, and you feel the world is yours. Not quite however, there's one final test. Pick up a couple or three cans, and stand them in the corner. Retreat to the distance of your farthest accuracy and take aim. When you can knock the cans over, or come reasonably close, your long kill is ready for use.

Whatever your degree of allegiance to practice, remember the value of the kill is twofold. It's a sure rally ender when executed properly and also serves as a tremendous morale booster. Regardless of whether you're winning or losing, there's nothing quite like being known as the guy or gal "with the kill."

48

CHAPTER 10

Pass on by

ALTHOUGH IT'S tempting to fire kills most every opportunity, success invariably comes to those who wait. But there are many occasions when a rally can be ended without the use of a kill. The strokes most often applied to fit the bill are known as passing shots.

Stroked from either the fore- or backhand these shots are the novice's best friend. The kinship is easily derived. A primitive proficiency with either stroke is sufficient to employ a shaky but functional pass.

Passing shots serve the function for which they are named. Whenever a shooter happens upon an occasion in which an opponent is out of position, the pass shot should come to mind. Why not? after all, what is more logical than hitting the ball where the opposition ain't (apologies to baseball fans and Wee Willie Keeler).

There are two basic forms of passing shots, the down-the-line, and crosscourt (see diagrams). Each works best under certain conditions. Whenever your opponent is standing to the far side of center court while you're positioned near the opposite side wall, the time is right for a down-the-line-pass.

Whether you're firing from the fore- or backhand

Pass shots are contacted higher than the kill shots; usually at knee to waist level. Picture here, the forehand (left) and backhand (right) strokes.

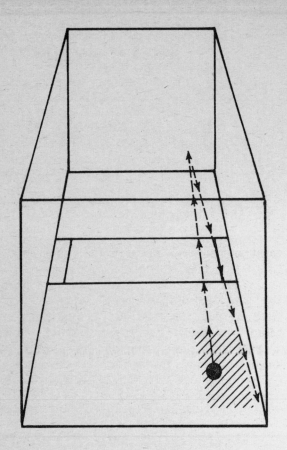
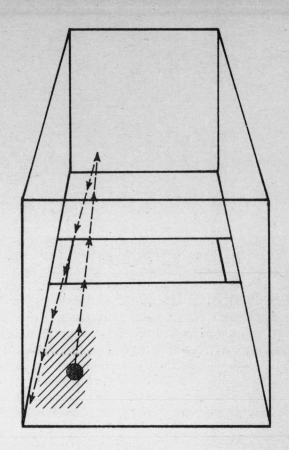

Down-the-line and crosscourt pass shots diagramed: Above—Down-the-line from the forehand (left) and backhand (right). Below—Crosscourt pass from forehand (left) and backhand (right) sides.

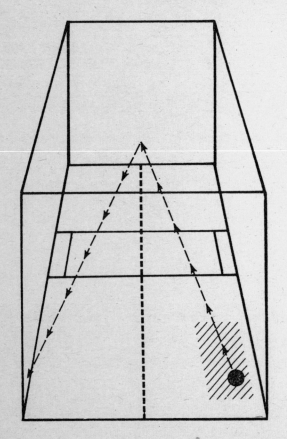
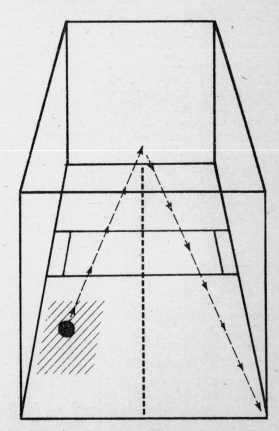

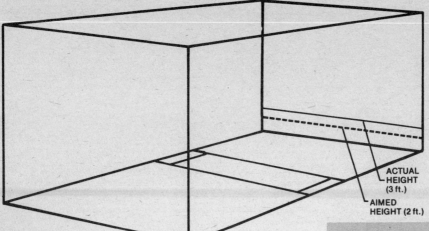

Left—Target area on front wall for pass shots is at about waist level (about 3 feet). Aim a bit lower to compensate for tendency of ball to gain altitude after it is struck.

Below—Rear view of down-the-line pass to the left side. If opponent is behind and to the right, the time is ripe for a pass to the backhand.

ACTUAL HEIGHT (3 ft.)
AIMED HEIGHT (2 ft.)

side, listen closely. Aim for a spot about waist high on the front wall. Stroke the ball firmly as you want it to rebound off the wall and carry down to the far corner. When hit correctly the ball will take its second bounce prior to reaching the back wall. This second bounce is an important aspect as it deprives the opponent of a reprieve courtesy of the back wall. The ball should pass by the opponent before he has had much time to move. It should never hit a side wall prior to reaching the corner area. Most times a well-hit pass will end the rally. There will be moments however when the opposition will make an exceptionally good return. No need to worry though. At the very least the return will force the opposition out of center court position. With a little more luck the return will be a plum you immediately can harvest.

There will of course, be instances when you and your opponent will reverse the previously described positions. The reader will be to one side in midcourt with the opposition nearby. Whenever this situation arises think crosscourt pass.

As with the down-the-line, you want to aim for a waist-high point on the wall. This point should be about midway between your position and the sidewall opposite the opponent. When the shot is contacted properly the ball will react much like the down-the-line, and speed toward the back corner. This shot is versatile and presents several options for use.

Picture yourself stationed at three-quarter court. Your opponent is in front to a side and has hit a returnable drive up the middle—a mistake. Regardless of which side the ball steams toward, get ready to fire and reap. But be careful of your aim in this circumstance. Using the waist-high range (or slightly lower) try to plant the ball a foot or more to the far side of front wall center. If you're on target the ball will fly in the path of a "V", bouncing off the far side wall. This shot is deadly in more ways than one. If, and it's a slim one, the returner manages to scamper backwards in pursuit, the rebound off the side is bound to throw him or her off bal-

Every now and then a pass shot will fly off the racquet and strike the wall lower than intended—the result is a rollout kill.

ance. Second, the shot can be hit with such speed the ball often bypasses the returner before he or she has time to blink.

When developing this shot, don't frown in disgust if the tail-end of the "V" doesn't always bounce off the side wall. As long as the shot bypasses the returner in front court it will likely prove a winner.

Practice

One of the more beneficial aspects of passing shots is that they are extremely simple to practice. Whether you're hitting from the forehand or backhand try these simple yet effective drills.

Walk to about three-quarters court to the side of your choice. For our purpose let's assume the forehand or right side (lefties read "ouch," left side). Assume the ready position, drop the ball and aim away. For the down-the-line shots try to hit the spot that carries the ball downcourt without brushing the side wall. For the crosscourt aim at the mid-point, again waist high, and watch the "V" in flight. After you've repeated this exercise several times, move up to half-court and repeat the same. Then move a little closer. When you start to tire of the drill, stroke the shots off a ball hit off the wall. For a challenge, stand in midcourt, throw the ball off the front wall to either side, and pursue with vigor. Don't forget to hit an equal share of down-the-line shots.

Before beginning practice lock this tidbit away for future reference. As far as beginners are concerned it's equally profitable to stroke passing shots from the backhand side. Try to concentrate on passes to the opponent's backhand. Most players' forehands—even

the most advanced—are apt to be more deadly than their backhand.

Hence the recommended shot is a crosscourt pass to the left-hand or backhand side (once again, lefties read right). By following advice the shooter will force the opponent to use the less proficient shot and maximize chances of a less aggressive return.

By the way, another variation of the crosscourt pass is the wide "V" pass. Use this stroke when you're in deep side court and the opponent is front and center. Aim for a waist-high point midway on the front wall and let 'er rip. Once again the ball will resemble a migratory fowl as it unerringly speeds to the far rear sidewall and corner.

After you become accustomed to stroking down-the-line and crosscourt passes, try this: Stand to one side at three-quarter court and hit a crosscourt pass. As the ball starts off on its "V" move to the opposite side of the court and bat back a like return. At first try to hit three consecutive crosscourts accurately, then move up the ladder. Do the same for down-the-line passes, but stay in roughly the same spot after contact.

A certain variation is likely to occur while practicing that will delight you. Every now and then a pass will fly off the racquet and strike the wall at a point lower than intended. Your eyes may feel like popping out of their sockets but relax, it's true, you've hit your first rollout kill. Whatever you do don't deliberately attempt another. You're sure to come up short.

Sometimes after hitting a rollout or bottom-board kill newcomers look upwards to see if their feat has been observed. If so, they may begin to sport the airs of a champion as they strut about court. Until they hit the next shot into the floor that is.

CHAPTER 11

Additional Ammunition

ALONG WITH THE passes, and kills there are other shots designed to help your offensive game plan. One of the most subtle yet effective is called the "drop" or "dump" shot. Strangely enough, this is a maneuver which can often be used to greater extent by beginners than top-level players.

The Drop Shot

The drop shot can be used when the shooter finds him or herself much closer to the front wall than the opponent. As the ball bounces off the wall, the racquet is extended forward, wrist cocked but firm. Barely flipping the ball with a still bent wrist the shooter dumps or nudges it softly toward the front wall. Due to the lack of power behind the shot, more often than not the ball will bounce twice before the opponent can successfully make the return.

One of the negative aspects concerning the drop shot is its frequency of use. Since its success is based on exploiting the position of the opponent, few foes are eager to be burnt twice. This means both eyes will be on the lookout should the situation repeat itself. If the returner correctly anticipates the drop shot there is little the hitter can do but start walking to the backcourt. Few players exist who are unable to stroke a winner off a knee-high ball bouncing toward them within 5 feet of the front wall.

This keen sense of anticipation developed by top

Left—The drop or dump shot. Use a stiff wrist to nudge the ball towards the front wall. Hit properly it should die after impact.

Below—Don't try the drop shot with a backhand. The ball will hit too high off the front wall.

ranked players works against their extensive use of the shot. But there's no reason why beginners should fail to make use of the stroke until their opponents wise up. One last point concerning the stroke—don't attempt it with the backhand. If you try you're likely to offer plum after plum off the wall.

As for practice, don't worry about it. Since many of racquetball's machinations are difficult to master, refrain from spending too much time on the drop. Once you develop the other shots sufficiently the ability to dump the ball often comes along for the ride.

The Overhead Drive

Another stroke which can be used in the offensive barrage is the overhead drive. Like the kill which rockets forward at a low trajectory, the overhead takes a fast but higher approach. All but an infinitesimal number of players strike the blow with the forehand for maximum impact. As with the passes, the overhead can be struck either down-the-line or crosscourt.

There are several reasons which mitigate against great use of this stroke. First, contact is made from above, with the impetus of the racquet arm, body and followthrough serving to bring the shot downward.

The point of contact on the wall should be about 1-foot off the floor. The path of travel followed by the ball when hit with too much gusto can be especially

disastrous. Instead of taking a second bounce from the front wall the ball may hit the back wall and stay alive, producing a ripe fat plum.

In order to hit the screeching overhead, the shooter engages in the following ritual. Standing at about three-quarter court (try to hit from the forehand side first) the hitter brings the racquet into an extended forehand backswing. The forearm is almost at a right angle with the upper arm, the racquet is pointing slightly floorward. Stepping up on the toes of both feet, weight largely on the right foot, the shot is about to be delivered. Extending the racquet arm forward, the racquet begins to raise as it nears the incoming ball. At the point of contact, the racquet has fully straightened. The momentum of the body weight transferred to the left foot, coupled with the racquet arm's extension and descent direct the ball floorward. After contact the downswing continues as the extended racquet arm moves further across the body. By the time the follow-through has been concluded most of the body weight is on the left foot while the racquet arm has sprawled across the width of the torso. This is not one of the sport's more graceful postures. In terms of effect, the three-quarter overhead is definitely one of the lesser used assets of the top-level player. From a viewpoint of effect however, the shot can be a worldbeater. Especially when facing a less-tenured opponent prone to be

Facing page and below—The overhead drive. This stroke can be used to deliver kills or low drives. Note the point where weight transfer takes place (second photo), right foot is up in air. Due to high angle of incidence, the ball will likely rebound high after striking front wall.

intimidated by the speed of a smoking overhead.

Beginners having little difficulty with the basic drives would do well to keep the overhead in mind. While you may find it surprisingly easy to cow another beginner with a bristling overhead drive, don't take it for granted against a veteran.

However, there have been a few times in the annals of racquetball when a defensive minded old-timer has been caught totally off-guard by a brash rookie. Parlaying an occasional overhead with good shot selection a newcomer can keep an opponent sufficiently off balance to win some points, and perhaps a game.

When such a matchup takes place each rally is contested on a physical and psychological level. While both players utilize various shots, the memory of that first screaming overhead remains in the veteran's mind. The novice isn't sure whether or not the bullet phased the opponent, but realizes it may have. The opposite number was surprised by the shot, but isn't sure whether or not it was a fluke. In any case, the interchange of uncertainties has benefited the less experienced player.

As long as the veteran has reason to fear a certain stroke of the opponent, he or she is apt to play a more cautious game. Whenever a player is able to instill caution or intimidate another, the shot employed is worth its weight in top-grade nylon string. Unless of course the beginner has chosen to bewilder the opposition with a display of masochism, stroking errant kill shots one after the other. Fortunately, few if any readers will probably pursue this tactic.

The Overhead Kill

There's one other use of the overhead that duty obliges the text to recognize. It's the overhead kill. Stroked like the drive, the shot is delivered from the forehand, and most always is sent crosscourt. Due to its inordinate velocity the shooter is best off sending the ball off the sidewall first (see diagram). The desired contact point off the side wall should be about 3 feet high.

The dangers inherent to this form of kill verge on the absurd for the newcomer. Not only is the ball struck from the backcourt, it's heading wallward at a downward incline. This makes it difficult to cleanly pinch the ball into the corner. Not only are the odds stacked against the shot working as a winner, it's also structured to perform ineptly as a passing shot. Then again, of course, there are numerous instances when the ball will bounce off the floor before striking the sidewall.

Thus far, each stroke has been analyzed from a common approach: that of orthodox preparation from an instructional perspective. As racquetball is a game of intense action and reaction there are going to be occasions however when the unorthodox is called for. Like, for instance, when an opponent's shot streaks directly toward you, without bouncing, after contact with the front wall.

During such a moment all the carefully studied and rehearsed practice sessions won't help a whit if you don't keep your head and react calmly. It may seem a trifle hard to believe but there's a whole school of court thought devoted to how best to cope with the onrushing sphere.

The Volley

Rather than have you shut your eyes on court, drop the racquet and flee, or protect yourself as well as possible, try a volley. The volley is the name given a variety of shots that have evolved consistent with the close confines and fast-pace of the game. Technically speaking, to volley is to hit the ball out of the air on the fly.

Based on the premise of aggressive defense (or self-preservation) a player should approach the rocketing ball with a confident attitude. Utilizing whatever stroke is called for, midair contact should be made following standard procedure. Whether forehand, backhand drive, overhead or kill, deliver the blow with your regular motion. Above all, be confident. There will be extremely few occasions when the ball will come upon you so rapidly it will knock the racquet from your hand.

When you're caught close to the wall and have no choice but to volley here's how to turn potential disas-

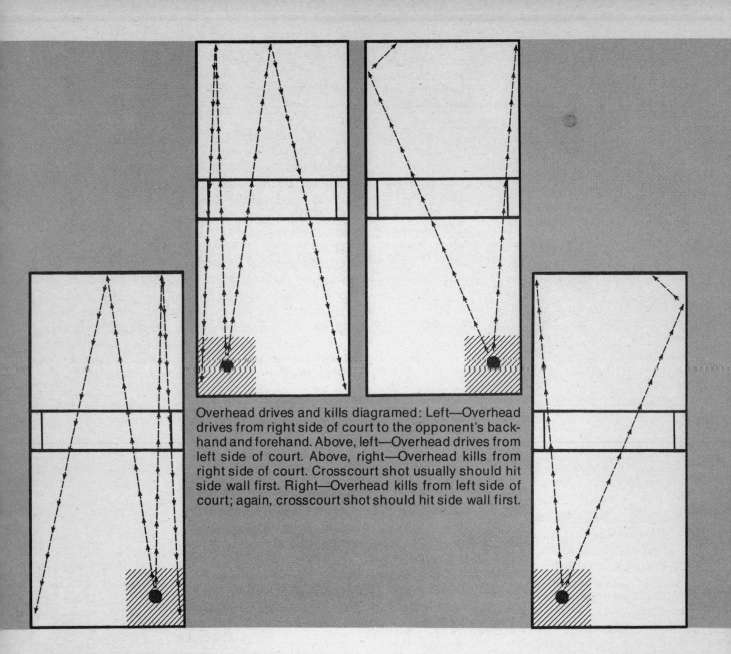

Overhead drives and kills diagramed: Left—Overhead drives from right side of court to the opponent's backhand and forehand. Above, left—Overhead drives from left side of court. Above, right—Overhead kills from right side of court. Crosscourt shot usually should hit side wall first. Right—Overhead kills from left side of court; again, crosscourt shot should hit side wall first.

ter into a windfall. Odds are at least even that your opponent is positioned much deeper on the court. In fact, the rocket hissing toward you may be a pass gone awry. Seize the opportunity to extend a stiff-wristed racquet to the ball, and dump the shot off the front wall. Carried out successfully the maneuver will accomplish two beneficial side effects. First, your ability to pick off a hard shot and render it impotent will cause the opposition to chastise itself for carelessness. It may, depending on his degree of experience, have an unsettling effect that can last for several rallies. A successful volley return of a front wall sizzler is also bound to boost your own confidence.

Not all volleys should be approached with an air of foreboding and mistrust. Believe it or not there will be times when you will look for and relish the opportunity to volley with abandon. It's worth remembering not all shots resemble comets with red-hot tails in their wakes.

For example, picture a lazy overhead, soaring in your direction. With a gleam in each eye you realize this is one easy ball to return for a winner. Leaping forward (always charge to volley, when possible) you proceed to deliver your first aggressive volley.

One thing to watch out for, though. It's fairly difficult to hit a low winner when the shot is taken overhead due to the angle of incidence. So, unless you want to try a tough shot off the ceiling, let the chance pass.

Once you get the hang of it it's easy to step aside in deep court, let the ball bounce, pop off the backwall, and step into a wicked off-the-wall shot.

If you're looking for a guide to which shots to volley, hone in on returns from knee-to-waist high. Operating within this range you should be able to return any shot with a reasonable facsimile of form and some extra power to boot.

Upon reaching this point it's come time to inspire you

as to the best way to practice the volley. It should go without saying it's unwise to stand near the wall and rocket balls in your own direction. On an encouraging note, most dumps off volleys come off reflex action.

As for the other more assertive volleys, here's what to do: Pick a place on court, say about even with the service line and hit yourself a soft, waist-high shot off the front wall. Make sure to stroke it hard enough that it doesn't bounce enroute to your position.

Be sure to move accordingly as the ball nears, and assume the proper setup position. Hit a series of 10 or so, alternating kills with passes, forehands and backhands. After you've stroked a score or two of these volleys, move back five paces and do the same. Then repeat the exercise from either side of the court. You may feel the urge to experiment with some other versions. Whatever the shot, repeat it with some degree of regularity and incorporate it into the practice routine.

Try to catch the opposition off-guard with a volley whenever possible. Make sure the shot is hit or aimed well enough that it doesn't bounce off unwanted walls. Why hand a life preserver to a floundering opponent?

There's one other version of the volley to enumerate. Half-baked by nature, the name follows suit—it's called the half-volley.

Picture the following scenario. You're standing at the back of the service box awaiting your opponent's return from the deep right-hand corner. The ball wafts off the front wall, weakly, the best that could be done with a good shot. The ball, traveling slowly to your forehand, looks like a textbook example of a perfect shot to volley for a winner.

Stepping forward confidently you prepare to unleash a streaking kill to the left-front corner. Only, suddenly you realize something's wrong. Instead of reaching you in mid-air the return is going to fall short. Anticipating a waist-high arrival you've moved too far back. Swooping downward the ball takes a short hop before you. What to do? You couldn't be more off-balance, and there's no time to setup again. There's only one answer, put forward a stiff upper lip and continue as planned. The result may be a superbly botched effort, but the chance exists your form (hopefully) will win the day. By carrying through normally with the half-volley to the tune of a probable sad ending you may reap unexpected benefits. Like the public speaker who missed a line but carried on convincingly, no one need know the shot was unplanned. In fact, there will be times (probably infrequent, and not worth fantasizing about) when an awkward half-volley will result in a rollout killer. It's up to you whether you grin knowingly, cry out in surprise, or nonchalantly take it in stride. Whatever your behavior, don't bother practicing the shot.

You heard right, don't waste much time drilling on the half-volley. Inasmuch as it resembles an aborted stroke your regular practice should prepare you for its use.

Above—A backhand volley. There will be instances when the ball comes upon you before bouncing off the floor. Address it with a stiffened wrist for a soft volley.

Below—A half-volley in progress. It's an aborted volley shot precipitated by a weaker than anticipated return by your opponent. The ball is taken after a short hop instead of on fly.

CHAPTER 12

Defense

UP TO THIS POINT the text has stressed material that featured the aggressive, offensive facets of racquetball. There's another side though that's equally important as the best way to stroke winners.

Before you leap into the fray and say "defense, who wants to hear about that?" reflect a moment. Far too often the concept of defense is portrayed in a negative, coyish light. Well, throw out any negative perceptions of defense as it relates to racquetball. Within the four-walled court, defense is a multi-faceted discipline. It's utilized to set up an offensive thrust as well as for point prevention.

Without the ability to play first-rate defense it is virtually impossible for any player to compete successfully oncourt. Defensive racquetball is a challenging and exciting aspect of play. With the tools for an adequate defense in hand, a player can pursue several strategies. He or she can seek to nullify opponent's strengths or move to exploit opponent's visible weaknesses.

Whichever tack is pursued, the defensive game should open the door for a show of offensive firepower. There will be times when the offensive game comes up short and fails to pass muster (or the opponent). During those moments both points and the game or match can be lost if the player can not rely on a defensive game plan. By fighting a delaying action the player can pick the best opportunities for offensive chances, capitalize on the opponent's mistakes and bolster confidence at the same time.

There will be occasions when neither you nor your opponent are aware of the other's strengths and weaknesses. Rather than rail wholeheartedly into the opposition's game you may choose to sample the firepower selectively. By using the defensive game you can force the opponent to deliver each of his or her strokes from a position suited to your best advantage.

From the description just unleased it might seem as if a veritable tool box of strokes is needed to play defense. Not so. In fact, the entire defensive game is based upon the use of only three. They are: the ceiling ball, the Z-ball, and the around-the-wall-ball. At this time a knowledgeable beginner is likely to blurt out loudly,

"Ah-ha, got yah, you forgot about the lob!" Well, not really. We'll get back to the lob later, but for now let's go with the assumption there's a debate concerning its use as a defensive measure.

The Ceiling Ball

Perhaps the most important of all defensive shots available is the ceiling ball. This is an extremely intriguing shot, from the viewpoint of spectators and players alike.

One of the most noticeable first impressions enjoyed by many observers is the fact that the ball is hit off the ceiling. The very fact that the ceiling is in play surprises many visitors. The surprise grows stronger as players stand in the backcourt and bat the ball off the ceiling to each other. Yet, after further observation there seems to be a method to the madness.

Sure enough, the repetition of roof-pounders eventually takes its toll on one of the participants. Perhaps through boredom, or an opportunity perceived by one of the players, the ceiling exchange is halted. Stepping firmly into the descent of the last roof-topper a player hits a hard straight shot toward the front wall. Moving forward quickly, just a step or two, the opponent returns the shot for an easy winner.

With a grimace of disgust the unfortunate aggressor retreats to backcourt to await the service. Without a moment's hesitation the service is returned via the ceiling, and the agony starts again.

This recounting may be slightly dramatic but the essentials are correct. By engaging an opponent with ceiling balls the hitter is forcing the opposition to reply in kind. Despite the idea that it looks easy to hit, appearances are deceiving. For all practical purposes, (and it's worth etching into the thinktank) the best way to return a ceiling ball is with another.

Properly stroked a ceiling ball is a creature of geometric beauty. Directed toward a spot on the ceiling roughly 5 feet or inwards from the front wall, it takes off on an intriguing journey.

Caroming abruptly off the roof it strikes high on the front wall and streaks downward, descending in the near backcourt. As it is struck with sufficient power to

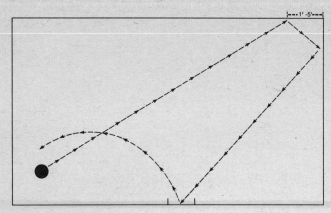

The ceiling ball diagramed: Left—Typical flight path. Aiming point is 1 to 5 feet from front wall. Below—Forehand and backhand ceiling ball trajectories. Bottom—Crosscourt ceiling ball from the forehand.

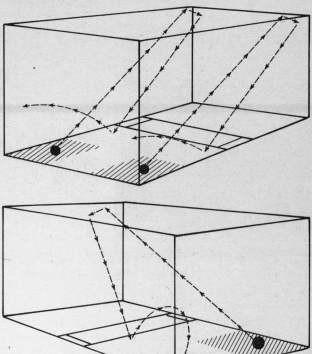

make the trip safely the rebound is invariably high, landing in deep backcourt. This facet serves to forestall many shot options the opposition would rather pursue.

In all likelihood you'll soon get the chance to engage in a ceiling ball rally and wait for an accident or error in judgement to take place. Patience is important in the ceiling game but the rewards more than justify the wait.

Now that the justification and rewards have been explained, it's time to examine the stroke itself. Most ceiling shots are hit with a three-quarter overhead motion, although there are certain times when a full overhead is employed. Picture yourself throwing a baseball. If you're not a fan of the national pastime, envision a serve in tennis. The same motion is used for the ceiling shot.

The first step to take in preparation is to note the path of the ball. As you'll likely be positioned near the back wall it's imperative several tasks be accomplished before the sphere's arrival. First, the racquet arm must be fully cocked behind the head prior to arrival.

Secondly the knees should be slightly bent, ready to propel the body in vertical climb. The weight should be mostly on the right foot (lefties, substitute left), although it will begin to transfer on impact. As the ball enters the immediate area, roughly 5 or so feet away, the racquet face should be almost parallel with the floor, so as to allow for maximum wrist snap. With the ball in range the racquet begins its ascent to the ball, guided by the helpful elbow held high. Swinging forward to smite the sphere the racquet impacts slightly in front of the body. Note how vertical the body is at this time, and the weight has neatly been transferred from the right to left foot. As the ball begins to take off skyward, the stroke continues through to completion. The wrist snap, begun immediately before contact continues on until fully uncoiled. While this action ensues the racquet arm continues its journey, finally terminating extended across the body.

Keep in mind the ceiling ball will be struck from approximately 30-35 feet deep on the court. Therefore don't nudge the ball when you greet it, deal it a hard enough blow to reach the deep back court at journey's end. By the same token there's no need to bludgeon the

ball either. Hit too hard, the ceiling ball can become the hitter's own public enemy number one.

How so? If the ball is struck too firm a blow it will follow the prescribed path, bounce sharply off the floor and proceed post-haste to the back wall. The ball will then rebound in a soft arc easily and eagerly welcomed by the opposition. Having stationed yourself in the backcourt, your fate is solely in the opponent's hands. With any luck, and concentration, you'll strive to prevent future occurrences. Also, don't forget the danger inherent in drubbing the ball too softly on a ceiling shot. Instead of bouncing harmfully off the backwall the shot will barely reach the backcourt before bouncing off the floor. Unless the opponent is comatose he or she will note the dying flight and rush forward to say hello. Once again there's little chance you'll get another turn at the ball during the rally.

A commonly asked question concerning the ceiling ball has to do with the construction of the court. "As there are two corners, isn't there a need for a backhand ceiling ball too?" The question is an apt observation, deserving a prompt response.

Yes, there is such a creature as a backhand ceiling ball, but it tends to produce difficulty for beginners.

That difficulty, however, is by no means relegated exclusively to first timers. While the backhand stroke

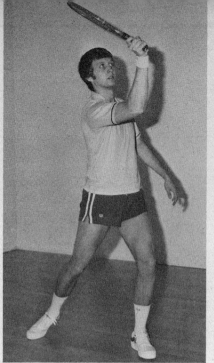

Overhead stroke for the forehand ceiling shot. Racquet starts out about parallel to floor with elbow held high. Weight is transferred from back to front foot and wrist is snapped smartly.

seems initially unnatural to many players, the thought of a backhand ceiling shot borders on the supernatural. Here's why it constitutes such a dilemma. In our examination of the backhand drive and kill it was made clear the racquet face must be perpendicular to the floor at the moment of impact. Only by attaining this perpendicular relationship with the floor can the ball be directed in a clean, straight line of flight.

The backhand version of the ceiling ball however forces the shooter to greet the ball with a slightly open racquet face (the top of the racquet slightly back of perpendicular).

Despite the difference, the individual should still seek to employ the fundamentals of the backhand stroke. There are several deviations however. The preliminaries to the stroke begin as imagined with the hitter stepping sideways well in advance. All remains normal as concerns some other critical checkpoints. The knees bend slightly, and body weight rests on the left foot (substitute, lefties). The racquet arm is cocked and resides in the setup position near the left ear. Here's where things tend to get a little chancy beginners, so read closely.

The trick to the whole shebang is to swing your hips around towards the back wall. Be sure to move in a leftwards fashion as a rotation to the right would leave you hopelessly contorted.

As this spring-like action is completed, the body weight lies in almost total repose on the left foot. This is a very power oriented stance, ready to bolt forward at the ball. Keep tabs on the shoulder of your racquet arm at this time.

In order to maximize the stroke's delivery system for a lusty swipe, be sure to tuck or secure the shoulder inward.

With this adjustment the player's frame is ready to unload upon the ball with the utmost efficiency.

As the blow is being delivered, the ball should be about head high, while the lead foot (the right) has taken a 45-degree step towards the side wall. As this step is taken the body has transferred most of the weight onto the right foot. This shift comes courtesy of the healthy unwinding of the hips and knees from their previously coiled posture. Striking the ball with the open racquet face the orb has little choice but to head toward the fifth wall (the ceiling).

After impact it's important to note the followthrough. The racquet arm continues to extend away from the body towards the ceiling. As with the forehand be careful to hit the ball with sufficient, but not too much or little power.

Don't be depressed at first if your backhand ceiling balls fly directly upward, strike the ceiling and fall to the floor. It's a more than common experience, and one that practice will eventually cure.

Although it may take time to develop the ceiling shot, it's very important that the effort be made. Unlike other shots whose frequency of use is largely a matter of choice, the backhand ceiling ball falls into another category. Thinking opponents will generally try to place their ceiling shots to your backhand. Even the most unimaginative reader can foresee the difficulties that will arise in constantly trying to return these shots with a forehand delivery. Thus, despite an easy distaste for

Backhand ceiling ball usually produces difficulty for beginners.

the stroke, the backhand ceiling ball ranks as an unfriendly notion you'll have to strike a truce with.

There will be occasions when the player needs to connect on a ceiling ball with a full-overhead swing. The way to strike the blow is to continue through with a regular three-quarter stroke. The only difference you'll have to note concerns the incline of the racquet face. Whereas with the former the face refrains from pointing skyward on contact, the latter does so.

When attempting to handle a backhand ceiling ball delivered above the head things change somewhat.

Facets that remain the same are the sideways setup and the coiling of the hips and knees. When the ball approaches the hitter's vicinity these bodily parts continue on their normal course, except for the racquet arm. Since the ball must be met at a higher level, some adjustments are required.

In lieu of the crisp wrist snap used to propel the backhand ceiling ball, the orb is met with a stiff-wristed approach. After contact another deviation occurs. The followthrough is directed toward the floor as opposed to the ceiling.

These differences in technique are predicated by the undue height at which the ball was contacted. Utilizing an orthodox approach on a ceiling ball met overhead would be an exercise in futility. Each time contact was made the ball would inevitably rise straight upward, hit the ceiling and land at the shooter's feet.

You're about to encounter words which may seem uninviting, but grin and bear them. Before any of the ceiling balls can be mastered more than a goodly share of practice must be devoted to the pursuit. Although

many of the game's other shots may appear more dramatic in nature or dynamic in motion, few are as vital as the ceiling ball. Keep that view in mind as you run through the following drills.

Since both the forehand and backhand ceiling balls are directed towards the same purpose these exercises are indigenous to both.

Begin by standing in the backcourt, about 35 feet deep in the forehand corner. Throw a ball off the ceiling towards the front wall and get ready to hit the return as it descends. Try to return the ball to the point of origin. Once (and if) it homes back to your position, repeat the shot. Continue in like fashion until you can control the stroke with a high degree of accuracy.

Once you've mastered the forehand, or grown tired, or frustrated, move to the backhand side and repeat the drill. Remember, the trick is to pin the opponent in the backcourt, preferably in a corner.

No matter how much you'd rather work on other aspects of your game, hit another series of ceiling balls. Regardless of the boredom it'll be worth it when you're able to compete with and dominate play against your peers.

Having waded through what could be termed the agony of the ceiling ball, it's time to take a gander at one of the game's more amusing, and amazing shots.

The Z-Ball

It's called the Z-ball, and it's difficult to imagine any other facet of the game so beguiling to witness. The best way to observe the eccentricity of the Z-ball is to have one stroked at you. As that avenue is not directly forthcoming, the following word picture will have to do.

Viewed from above, the Z-ball is reminiscent of a ball in a pinball machine. Starting from the racquet face it speeds towards either side of the front wall and on contact caroms to the nearby side wall. Flying off at an oblique angle crosscourt it moves towards a sidewall

Properly aimed Z-ball allows shooter to scramble to center court position while forcing opponent into corner.

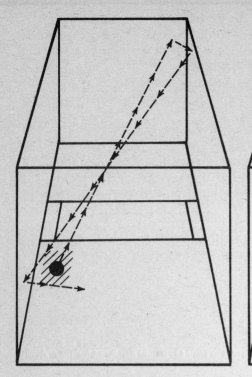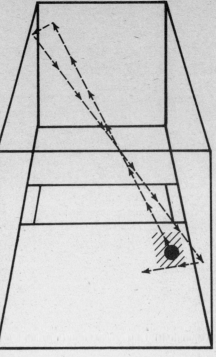

Left—Paths of backhand (far left) and forehand Z-balls diagramed. Below—Targets for forehand and backhand shots are 3 feet in from side wall and 3 feet down from front wall.

BACKHAND Z TARGET

FOREHAND Z TARGET

collision in the backcourt, with the ball clearly the loser.

Suffering from its prolonged travel the ball rebounds from the side wall and engages in a curious practice. Instead of heading backwards toward the back wall as would be expected, the battered sphere takes a perpendicular course towards mid-court. No, that wasn't a typo. It really takes a right angle bounce after impact.

Whatever else you may come to think about the Z-ball, there's one perspective that shouldn't be overlooked. How many other shots do you know of that have made a contribution to the world of athletic science fiction?

Before continuing with the examination of the Z-ball it's quite possible some readers have a few questions to ask.

Of all the queries, perhaps the most obvious asks "why does the ball bounce in such a weird fashion?" Without a degree in physics, it's difficult to scientifically answer the question. Albeit it's a good one. What can be said is despite the bizarre machinations of the Z-ball it's one of the easiest shots to master. In fact most any newcomer can step on court the first time, be shown where to aim, and "Z" to their heart's content.

To make the prospects even more palatable the Z can be stroked with relative ease with either the fore- or backhand.

There are specific areas from which it's most desirable to hit a Z-ball. This may startle you, but about the only stricture is that the hitter should be stationed off to a side and near the shortline.

As soon as that point is clear it's time to set the dervish in motion.

Stationed to the right (for the sake of illustrating the forehand) take a visual fix on the left hand side of the front wall. Focus on the corner, about 15-16 feet high. Once the logistics have been fixed, strike a firm forehand blow to the target region. If your sighting and stroke are in sync the ball should proceed nicely along its frenzied route (see diagrams).

Beginners generally fall in love with the Z-ball. When a novice armed with the Z is paired against an unwitting peer the results can be hilarious. Equal in most other respects a dose of Z-balls can quickly turn the tables.

Once the initial mortification has been endured, however the shot tends to lose much of its mystique.

Since the Z tends to perform with almost certifiable predictability those suffering prolonged exposure are quick to pick up its secrets. Instead of lurching about like a racquet-wielding Ichabod Crane a suddenly-experienced player simply struts toward where the ball should descend. Knowing both where and how the ball will bounce makes it easy to execute a safe return. In spite of this knowledge, the bizarre nature of the shot tends to limit the variety of returns. Most players are content to return a passable ceiling ball.

The Z has another useful purpose which is decidedly more defensive in nature. During rallies against top-flight opposition there are going to be times when it's difficult to make a stylish return. Rather than serve up a plum-like pass or kill the circumstance is perfect for a Z. In addition to the possibility that it may produce a winner, there's one thing it's sure to do—due to its extensive orbit it should provide sufficient time for you to regain balance and establish center court position.

There are a couple of things to watch out for when dishing up those flawless Z's. Don't ever hit the ball so high it glances off the front wall to the ceiling. The result will be a D-ball, named for the disastrous plum you've just served up.

Be careful the shot strikes the front wall within 3 feet or less of the corner you're aiming at. If it lands any closer to the middle of the wall the Z will rebound off the midway point of the sidewall. You guessed it, another "D-ball." It's also bad news if the Z is hit too hard and rebounds off the backwall for an easy setup.

Now that you're versed in the ins and outs of this lively stroke go and practice a few. Just pick a spot on either side of the service box and flail away. Try to vary your strokes with each series of five shots. The chances are excellent you'll soon be showing the shot to your friends.

Oh yes, don't be afraid to use the backhand version. It's called the Reverse Z.

Speaking of good things, there's an old saying they come in bunches. Well, two don't necessarily rate as a bunch, but the next shot is every bit as much fun as the Z-ball. Like the Z it has a funny name, travels a tricky route, and is helpful in a pinch. The Z gets its name from the path it traces about the court. The same holds true for the next shot which races around the walls. Any guesses as to the name?

The Around-the-Wall Ball

If you didn't go with your first impression you're probably wrong. It may not be creative but the creature is called the Around-the-Wall ball. Hearing this information readers may wonder aloud, "isn't the Z-ball an around the wall ball?" Yes, it is, but there are two differences between the strokes: The around-the-wall-ball (ATWB for short) is even simpler to hit than

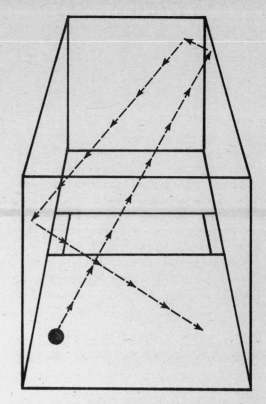

Diagram of the around-the-wall ball from the backhand side. Forehand version is the exact opposite of this flight path.

the Z-ball. The other difference lies in the fact that the side wall is first contacted by the speeding rubber bullet.

The shooter should stand to one side well behind the shortline and aim for a spot 3 feet from the front corner of the far (right) side wall. With a backhand stroke hit the mark about 15-17 feet high, and the ATWB is off to the races.

Rebounding off the right side it will strike the front wall, and travel obliquely to the opposite (left) side wall. Upon reaching its latest destination about mid-court and high on the wall, it will begin to show signs of fatigue. This aspect of the flight plan becomes visible as the ball begins a severe angular nosedive touching down around three-quarter court. Upon contacting the floor, the ball revs up and more or less gyroscopes high towards the rear right side wall. Faced with either volleying the ball as it descends from the left side wall or chasing after the rebound the returner is hard put for an answer.

By the way, this shot can also be stroked with equal success from the forehand side, however it comes off the right sidewall to your opponent's stronger forehand.

Like the Z-ball the ATWB can initially befuddle opponents but they'll soon catch on to its quirks. There are times, however, when it's most helpful. Such as when a desperation shot is required to continue a rally. Easy to hit it also provides the shooter with plenty of "scrambling time" to get back into position. There will also be instances when you're unhappy with the tempo of play. A prompt deployment of a series of ATWB's will change the pace nicely.

When stroking the shot there are some pitfalls to avoid. As with the Z make sure to keep the ball from striking the ceiling. It's also imperative to avoid, repeat avoid, hitting the ball with such force that it caroms high off the backwall. The majority of such mishaps will be converted into winners by the opposition.

Practice the ATWB in the same manner as the Z. Stand off to a side far behind the short line, aim and fire. Work on hitting the same spot each time. Begin by bouncing the ball to yourself, then hit caroms (drives or ceiling balls) coming off the wall. Keep on firing until you achieve consistent results then shift to the backhand. Remember to always practice stroking from both sides as you want to be able to attack fore- and backhand sides at will.

The Lob

At this time it's only correct to explain the controversial statement made earlier concerning the lob. The lob is a shot which is stroked high off the front wall over the head of the opponent. It is generally directed down the line, in the hope it will expire before reaching the backwall. Granted, by the basis of this description it appears to be a totally reputable defensive weapon. Certain aspects of the shot however tend to mitigate against its use as a defensive tool.

A major objection to its employment lies in the ease with which it can be mishit. Today's racquetballs are lively items and carry readily to the back wall if stroked too hard. Secondly, the shot is difficult for beginners who not only have to aim correctly, but must judge the speed of the ball and position of their opponents. Too hard a hit results in a back wall plum. Too soft and the opposition can pound away at an easy overhead volley. Third, and perhaps the telling point, why bother with these imponderables when the ceiling ball easily meets the need?

Those readers who have heard great things about the lob shouldn't feel defeated or deflated. Some of the best players use the lob because they have the refined skills to utilize it effectively.

Defensive Strategy

We've now gone over the majority of defensive shots utilized in racquetball. Readers about to play for the first time or those seeking additional information should consider the following: No matter how impressive a game an opponent may have, resist the desire to copy another's style. Work within the boundaries of your own abilities and build upward. There are certain traits, however, which are universal to top play—especially defense. First and most inviolate, never relax on defense. Each time you mishit a return one of two things

can happen, both bad. Either you lose a point or surrender the service.

When you're situated in a defensive posture strive to always keep the ball in sight. The analytical abilities of an Einstein aren't required to deduce that shots unsighted will rarely be returned.

Assuming your remain vigilant there are a few tactics you can employ to best serve your ends. The paramount objective of defense is to prevent the opposition from controlling play. This can be accomplished by denying access to the center court area. Each time you stroke a shot watch your opponent's reaction and timing. Pick your shots accordingly so that the opposition spends the majority of time in the backcourt. When the moment is right you can assume center court dominance.

Most new players should only employ those defensive strokes in which they have confidence. Practice is the time to develop new wrinkles and iron out flaws. Do your best to develop a healthy ceiling game. Many individuals however, find it unnatural and irksome (not to mention just plain hard) to stroke the ball off the ceiling.

This frame of reference is readily understood. Most persons are drawn courtward with thoughts of becoming a part of the action. Action that includes rapid fire kills and drives, not high shots lofted off the roof. Matches between novices often feature little else but a series of drives and kills with nary a ceiling or Z-ball to be seen. These contests are fun to play but will rarely lead toward development of the participant's potential.

It's also wise to approach an opponent you've never played from a surgical perspective. Utilizing your entire repertoire of shots, seek out the foe's weak and strong points. A few points may be lost in the process, but sooner, rather than later, you'll have discovered the chinks. Once you're certain, utilize defensive shots to force errors you can exploit offensively. Maybe that's what's meant by the phrase the best offense is a good defense.

One last word about the "other" defensive shots: The Z-ball and ATWB. Don't make the mistake of flocking exclusively to their banner due to easy learnability. No matter how you try to avoid it, the ceiling ball is one of racquetball's fundamental facts of life.

Oh yes, many times you may be obsessed with a sudden urge to fire a kill from the backcourt. Think three times about it. Devote the first thought to who's serving the ball, the next to court position and the last to the score. It may not sound defensive, but keep in the mind the adage about going forth into stormy seas. All things considered strive towards being able to play a competent, aggressive style of defense. Have the patience to wait for your opportunity, and seize it immediately. If you're beginning it may seem an impossible request, but think again. Given time and practice there's little doubt you'll acquit yourself admirably.

CHAPTER 13

Serving It up

Prime court position plus the time and opportunity to assess opponent's position give server a healthy advantage over the returner.

DEBATE MAY RANGE over a host of topics associated with racquetball but there's one which broaches no dissent. Each rally begins with the service. Properly executed the serve can terminate the rally or set the stage for a winning shot. Before analyzing the means by which these ends can be served (excuse the pun) let's examine the philosophy governing the service.

For purposes of recollection the service is the procedure through which the ball is put in play. Once the ball has been served a rally is said to have begun. Rallies are terminated when the ball fails to reach the front wall on a fly, or cannot be returned before it bounces twice. A less than quick wit can discern the fastest way to conclude a rally following a legal serve is by a mishit of the return.

Reasoning along those lines it behooves the server to do his or her best to cause the returner difficulty. The basic structure of the game aids the server in this endeavor.

Judged on strategic position alone the server enjoys a healthy edge over the servee. This advantage can appear overwhelming. Here's a brief balance sheet stressing the inequities: The server is situated on prime territory; the location of his or her choice within the lush center court service zone. The opponent stands in the backcourt far removed from center court. A little arithmetic helps clarify the differential. The server stands within 15-20 feet of the front wall. The opponent is stationed 30-35 feet away.

Prior to serving the individual has up to 10 seconds to put the ball in play. During this period the server is free to deliberate over a choice of serves and to evaluate the opponent's position. While the server mentally debates, the returner can do little but wait for the chance to react. As the seconds pass before the serve is initiated the anxiety factor can work against the returner. The server knows precisely when and what type of serve will be delivered—the opponent does not, hence there is a tendency to outthink one's self trying to predict the serve.

As the game proceeds and the players begin to recognize assets and deficits, this pre-serve deliberation continues to work against the returner. Having illustrated chinks in the armor, the returner is aware of his vulnerability. As such the pre-serve anxiety increases. The ball will either be served to attack a weakness, or served to a stronger area if the returner is given to overcompensating.

When it comes to weapons-at-hand the server is well-armed. Virtually any player, regardless of experience, can employ a wide-range of serves. There are four fundamental serves which can be classified as two knives and a pair of blunt instruments. They can variously be used to hit the ball at a high speed, force the opponent to utilize either his fore- or backhand, trap the foe in a corner, or minimize return opportunities.

Then again, the serve can always be attempted as an ace in its own right. Whatever the intent, the ability to

Above and opposite page—Forehand drive serve begins with ball bounce and racquet in ready position. With racquet arm back, body begins to lean into shot.

serve well is one of the most valuable assets a player can possess.

Now that the basic advantages have been stated, let's move to the various serves themselves. Before doing so, beginners should etch the following into their minds. Without a doubt the two most important shots in the game are the service and its return. Ideally speaking each point could be won by the server hitting an unreturnable ace. More likely though, a good serve will cause the opponent some grief, producing a poorly stroked return. Seizing the opportunity the rally should be won by the server.

As stated earlier the server has four basic tools that can be used. They are the drive serve, garbage (or half-lob serve), Z-serve and lob serve. Each can be employed toward a different end. It's nice to be able to control them all.

While each serve retains a character all its own some are definitely more intimidating than others—especially for beginning and intermediate players. Let's initiate the inspection with the most feared of all, the low drive to the backhand.

The Drive Serve

Judged by any standards, the low drive is a wicked, evil-looking shot. Picture a speeding rubber orb flying toward the backwall corner at a velocity well in excess of 100 mph. As the blur passes by it's traveling roughly 1 foot off the floor. Many newcomers wince physically upon hearing the sound of impact with the server's racquet. A momentary paralysis often sets in which further prevents a good return.

The ability to clout this intimidator can help in more ways than one. It can be used as a potential ace, especially if the opponent is slow afoot. The low-drive is also a wage-earner from the viewpoint of psychological damage inflicted.

There's no easier way for a game to be lost in the early going than for a player to be terrified of an opponent's serve. Even if the server has little confidence in the accuracy of his low-drive, the speed alone can significantly distress the opposition. What's best about the serve, and worth a few huzzahs from the envious is that it's easily learned.

Basically speaking the low-drive serve is executed in the manner of a forehand kill.

The low-drive is initiated with the server positioned sideways in the middle of the service box. (Before beginning, it's wise to glance backcourt and note the position of the opponent.) Moving into a slight crouch, the server drops the ball slightly in front of the body and begins the orthodox approach. Points to note are the following:

One—the ball must be struck no higher than knee level. There's a good reason as the target area on the front wall is roughly 3 feet high and 1 foot to the left or right of center.

Two—when you're about to unleash the low-drive, cast off the Clark Kentish elements of your personality and let the Superman (or woman) shine through. Hit the ball a powerful blow, but never so much you lose control.

Three—stay as low as you can throughout the shot. The key to the low-drive lies in the ability to deliver a

Racquet is moved forward rapidly while weight is transferred to front foot. After ball contact at knee level or below, follow through carries on smoothly.

Below—Drive serves diagramed. Note center court starting position with option of serving to opponent's forehand or backhand.

devastating shot that will angle low and true to the back corner. To maximize your power potential, picture the body as a spring coiling and unwinding. Imagine yourself wound into a crouch, you begin the recoil, moving forward with rapidly building momentum. Meeting the ball firmly off the left foot (sorry lefties) the follow-through continues onward with the racquet arm extending across the body.

Four—get ready to adjust quickly after the serve has been delivered. You should have some idea as to how the opponent will return the shot. Make sure you're in center court position, poised and ready to move forward or back as needed.

Once you've mastered the fundamentals of the low-drive it's best to practice alternate usage to both fore- and backhand sides. The front wall target areas are similar and require little adjustment from the service zone. When serving to your opponent's backhand, it may seem natural to step slightly towards the left of center. It's okay but try to avoid it as a rule. There are two reasons against, one of which, incidentally, is a rule in its own right. Anytime the serve rebounds so close to the server's body it obscures vision a screen call can be made. This means that the service must be replayed. Many readers grew up calling such replays "do-overs" in similar sports.

Secondly, in the rush to exploit the opponent's backhand, undue motion to the left works against the server. Not only does it telegraph intent, but places the server out of position should the return be a cross-court pass.

The projected path of the ball is also worth studying.

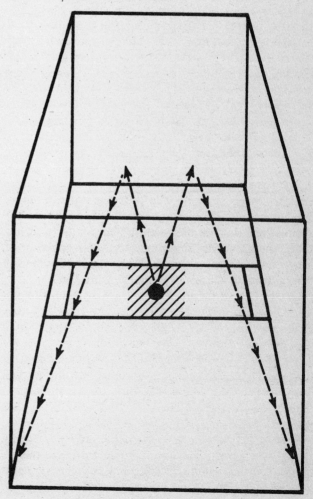

After contact has been made the ball should throb unerringly toward the rear corner. On certain occasions it will pass close to the side wall, bounce and ricochet softly off the back wall.

On others the ball will hum along near the rear side wall and actually tick it. This rub will prompt the sphere to shoot toward center court. Before the thought forms that's certainly a no, no, t'aint necessarily so. As long as the ball nips the sidewall within a foot or two of the corner, all will be well. The trajectory will form a near right angle with the side wall, producing a difficult return.

Disaster strikes, however, when the ball plunks the side wall far ahead of the corner. Slicing toward center court the ball undergoes a metamorphosis from rubber to fruit. Inasmuch as everyone likes sweets, the plum will be eagerly devoured.

There's another facet worth retaining before unlimbering your low-drive howitzer. A word to the wise, though—peruse the material to follow, consider it thoughtfully, but don't use it in a game if you're a beginner.

The Wide-V Serve

The subject is a variation of the low-drive serve called the wide-V. Technically speaking the low-drive we have been examining is labeled a center court narrow-V drive. It derives the label logically as the ball strikes near the front-wall-center and follows a "V" like path. By any standards the wide-V is a gamble. To stroke the shot the server remains in the center of the service zone but aims well to the side of the front-wall-center target. If all goes well the ball will pop off the front wall and proceed downward at an angle. It's headed toward a precarious rendezvous: a juncture just past the short line where the side wall meets the floor. If it arrives it will squirrel away at an unhittable angle. At least that's the projected ideal. What transpires most of the time is a result of a differing order. Lacking the geometric precision needed to wedge into the "bullseye" the ball hits slightly high on the sidewall. Rebounding, it flies unerringly to center court for an easy setup. Or it may hit the floor before the sidewall and glance off harmlessly, another sure loser.

Although the wide-V may appear to have been trampled over in the text, when executed properly it's a brilliant stroke. For beginners though, the shot should be avoided in competition like the plague. Anytime your practice sessions begin to reek with tedium, try a few wide-V's. As your drives improve with time, so will the accuracy needed to make the wide-V efficient.

Incidentally, you're likely to notice most every club has its own master of the low screaming drive serve. Wielding the serve like a weapon, the hard hitter usually is envied off court and is feared on court. Now there's nothing wrong with possessing confidence in one particular serve, but to use it exclusively is a step in the

Backhand service is not as common as the forehand variety, but it's wise to develop the stroke for the sake of varying serves.

wrong direction. Many times this truth will be discovered the hard way, against top-level opposition. Able to pick off the predictable serves with impunity—the opponent will ravage the server with passes and ceiling balls galore. Unaccustomed to being on the defensive the club's golden boy or girl will quickly lose some of the luster.

By the way, players utilizing backhand strokes on their drive serves are fewer than far between. Nonetheless, if you're one of the minority, don't feel embarrassed or isolated. In the final analysis all that counts is effect. And if you can strike low-driving whistlers from the backhand keep em comin'.

The Z-Serve

Of the remaining three serves, none is as transfixing as the Z. Like the Z-ball used in a rally the shot is a composite of ricocheting angles and divergent bounces.

Once again, it's just about as easy to hit as its rallying relative the Z-ball. First off, use the same stroke employed for the forehand kill and drive serve. The only difference in approach is in the angle of attack. Whereas the low-drive is directed slightly off the front-wall-center, the Z-serve is directed toward the corner. For purposes of this discussion, there are two variations of

to chest height. Stiff-wristed contact with open racquet face is made from below the ball. Target is point on front wall about 8 to 10 feet high and 1 or 2 feet in from center.

inviting, kills are unwise from shoulder height, as are passing strokes. The best alternative is a ceiling shot for which the server has plenty of time to prepare. Of course, against inexperienced opponents many garbage serves will be met by futile down-the-line kills. With time the opponent will eventually learn the error of his or her ways. By that time, however, the game may already be out of reach.

As with all serves there are a list of observables to heed when putting out the garbage serve (pardon the pun). Make certain the shot is hit soft enough that it doesn't fly off the back wall after bouncing. It's also necessary to be sure the ball never contacts the near side wall until it is in the corner. Any earlier contact will cause the orb to softly waft toward center court. The opposition will cherish this rendition of the garbage serve as if it were the crown jewels or plums.

When stroking the shot remember the main intent is direction as opposed to impression. Act accordingly and refrain from either walloping the ball or trying to be too artistic. All that's needed is a firm forward prod with the racquet face. Gravity will take care of everything else. Sometimes an opponent will run up and hit the ball before it bounces. Chances are the server will lose the rally when this occurs. Avoid reoccurances by mixing up your serves.

Before we move to another area, file this fact away: the garbage is golden from either side of the court. Don't be afraid to serve to both the fore- and backhand side of your opponent. Even though you may feel peculiar dishing up a serve with such a lackluster appearance, keep the faith. You'll be surprised how bad a return can be hit off a garbage serve when the opponent has grown accustomed to hard drives and Z's.

The Lob Serve

The last of the serves up for consideration is the lob. As the Z-serve and Z-ball share some common traits, so do the lob and half-lob (garbage) serves. When considering the two varieties of lobs, be especially cautious when it comes to serving up a whole lob. There's a reason for this timidity—it's prompted by the route the ball must travel during flight. While the half-lob is allowed to contact the floor after striking the front wall, the lob bounces to a different routine. It's a two-wall number, like the Z, but with a crucial difference.

Whereas in the Z the ball crisply rebounds off a front and side wall, only the front is initially struck during the lob. Glancing high off the front wall the ball cascades downwards to the left (once again to the backhand side

Left—Lob serve's delivery is same as garbage serve; however, aim point is about 15 feet high and roughly 3 feet from center of front wall.

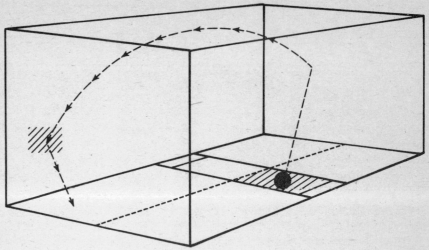

Above—Lob serve diagramed. Starting position is off-center in service zone; ball must nick the left side wall for serve to be effective. Pinpoint accuracy is a must with this shot.

for righties) in an effort to brush the side wall low in a backcourt descent. After ticking the side barrier the ball will spin off towards the back wall, making a return difficult. This shot has many obvious advantages in its behalf. It forces the opponent to the rear corner for the return, and the bounce is hard to handle. Unfortunately, its probable disadvantages carry approximately the same weight. If the ball fails to brush the side wall the results can be catastrophic. What takes place is a grim scenario where the returner calmly prepares a rocket-like pass or kill off the slow bouncing "super-plum." Then again, the serve can hit accurately, but with too much oomph behind it. When that occurs, the opponent gets the chance to tee-off on a slow-moving ball flying low off the backwall.

With the balance sheet evenly divided it's only fair to describe how an interested party can go about serving a lob.

Begin at center court, within the service zone (of course). Stand relatively upright, and firmly bounce the sphere off the floor. Move your racquet back as if you were going to hit a forehand drive. Wait until the ball starts to climb and begin to swing the racquet forward. The racquet should approach the ball from underneath, with the wrist held firm. The racquet face should be open on contact and the flow of the swing will carry the ball upward. Continue on with the follow through, guiding the racquet in the desired direction. The target area

on the front wall is roughly 1 to 3 feet left of center, and about 15 feet up.

While each player would love to have each serve described here at his or her disposal, it's not mandatory. Beginners should work on being able to consistently deliver a crisp serve and a softer version. It's especially easy to master the latter as the garbage serve is not finesse oriented.

When serving get the most out of each serve. Be sure to exploit an opponent's backhand to the maximum—doing so will probably unnerve and aggravate the opposition. With any luck this response pattern can work in your favor, à la a series of misguided kills and drives.

A note on practicing the serves. It can be extremely tedious to fire away, chase the ball down and walk back to the service line. However, it's more than necessary to develop a good service. So beg or buy a bucket of balls, or firm up your patience, but practice.

Each serve can be practiced by standing in varying positions in the service zone, aiming and hitting. After each serve check the locale. As always strive for consistency. Remember to serve to both the fore- and backhand.

If a friend is available, ask him or her to share in these drills. It's more enjoyable with two, and you don't have to chase the balls. Then again it never hurts the ego to see your wicked serves causing an opponent to flail the air wildly (you hope).

CHAPTER 14

Returning the Serve

UP TO THIS POINT we've examined many of the components that comprise the sport of racquetball. Studied individually each stroke possesses a life of its own and a set of circumstances that best governs its use. It's appropriate to analyze these circumstances and learn when to utilize which shot. The best place to begin naturally, is at the beginning, with the return of serve.

From the first moment you step into the backcourt an unspoken war of wits begins to germinate between server and receiver. In order to best do battle, it's important to establish the proper court position. To locate your starting block, stand in the backcourt, in line with the midpoint of the back wall.

Make sure to position yourself between 3 and 5 feet from this bullseye. In case you're not disposed to accurately judging distances, it translates to about a racquetarm's length from the back wall. Once you've got a fix on this spot, memorize it. It's your point of return whenever you're about to receive the serve.

Okay, you're established at said point, and have assumed the ready position. "What comes next?" is the question likely on your mind. That, readers, is in the hands and mind of the player in the service zone.

There are some cues you can remember however, to even out the odds. Generally speaking certain types of serves should beget specific returns.

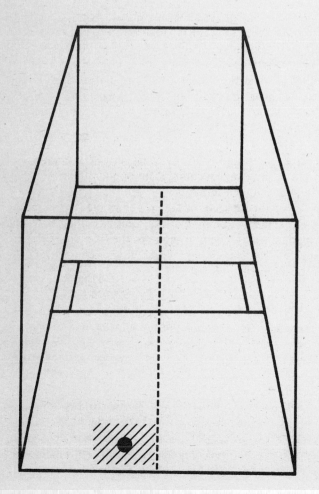

Above—Service receiver in the ready position.

Left—Starting position for service receiver is about a racquetarm's length from the back wall and either at court mid-point or slightly to left of it.

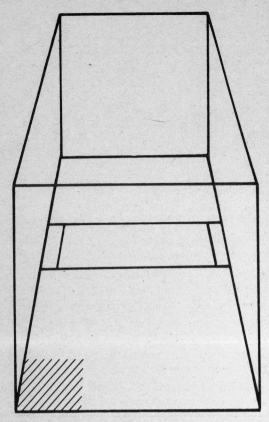

Above—The ceiling ball is the most logical return of a serve sent deep to a corner. Opponent is forced to evacuate center court position for the return—step up and seize it for your own.

Left—Basic strategy for serve returns is to direct your returns to your opponent's backhand in the back court—see shaded area.

Returning the Drive Serve

Let's begin with the drive serve and see where that takes us. We've already stressed there are several options the returner can pursue when chasing down a drive serve.

Thoughts of answering in kind with a bullet-crosscourt "V" or down-the-line pass readily leap to the fore. Highly aggressive players may think the moment right for a low pinch or straight kill return.

Despite the appeal of these shots the overwhelming choice of most players is a return of a more gentle nature: the ceiling ball. As the law of probability rules against sustained success with the low hard road the player should choose the highway of least resistance. That will most always be the ceiling. Following the fundamentals the returner should move smartly towards the ball set up sideways and shoot skyward. As your opponent evacuates center court for the return step up and seize it for your own.

If the opposition replies in kind, don't hesitate to send the next shot roofward also. If a game of ceiling chess ensues one of the players will crack first. A shot may hit the ceiling too far from the front wall and rebound to mid-court. A skyball may be shot too far to one side and strike the side wall on the path downward. In either case be prepared to attack with a low pass or kill shot.

Sometimes you'll find yourself making a mishit on the ceiling return and paying the price. Don't lose faith in

the tactic whenever such misfortune occurs.

While the ceiling ball is a logical return of a serve deep to a corner, players cannot be expected to function as robots. Whenever your opponent's drive serve fails to rocket towards the corner or squirts to the middle, change gears fast and return with a pass. When opportunity knocks seize the initiative—shun the ceiling ball and go for blood.

Avoid having your returns type cast and vary the pattern now and then. A sharp crosscourt pass will occasionally snap a complacent opponent out of a ceiling ball induced lethargy.

Be on the lookout for the proper moment to shoot the pass. After watching a succession of ceiling balls the opponent may begin to move to the backcourt prematurely. If you notice or sense the movement whiz the return of serve on by.

Returning the Z-Serve

It's likely you'll also spend time in pursuit of a Z-serve. The Z presents the returner with very few alternatives. Replete with sharp ricochets and weird bounces, it virtually cries out "ceiling ball, or else!" Beginners should be especially respectful and aim their returns skyward.

When setting up to return a Z-serve there are several details worthy of review. For starters, you'll be seeing a lot of Z-serves so get used to their puzzling flight plan. Remember the ball will hit two walls (the maximum allowed on the service) inflight and bounce deep near the opposite side wall. Be careful to avoid pursuing the path of the ball like a frenzied chicken. Respectful of the laws of geometry the Z-serve will always, repeat always, resolve its travels in roughly the same area. This knowledge of the flight plan can be put to good use. Make sure to position yourself properly and resist the temptation to merge into the side wall. Many times newcomers to the Z-serve will become obsessed with the flight of the ball and forget their positioning. Whenever this occurs the results are usually plumlike for the server; and embarrassing for the returner cramped in a corner. Remember there are two varieties of the Z-serve. One is hit a little higher and with less pizzazz than the other. Regardless of which comes towards you treat them accordingly, with a deft return to the ceiling.

Returning the Garbage Serve

Another serve you'll see a lot of is the garbage (or half-lob) serve. More than any other, the garbage begs the returner to take aggressive action. Waffling mid-range off the front wall the ball bounces slightly past the short line and proceeds along the side wall. As it progresses the returner is struck with the notion this is a terrific time for a drive and moves forward. But the ball is traveling at about shoulder height and it's hard to hit a drive from that location. A hasty reassessment is made, and a ceiling shot delivered. The server, in the meantime, has had plenty of time to get in position for a return.

Above and below—Server controls center court and the return should be directed to force server from choice spot. Here low drive serve calls for a crosscourt or pass return.

Then again, your ceiling shot (or lob perhaps) may be hurried and mishit. The server then finds him or herself ready to harvest another plum. The poorly stroked ceiling ball is likely to hit too far towards the rear of the ceiling and produce a midcourt plum. It may be hit too aggressively and bound weakly off the backwall.

What's paradoxical about the above return of a garbage serve is that the proper response is once again, a ceiling ball.

A difference in approach however, is the key. Aware of the garbage serve's deceptive appearance, the returner should be resigned towards issuing a ceiling retort. Stationed properly in advance of arrival, the returner should calmly stroke a skyball and begin the battle for centercourt position. In the earlier example describing a lunging, ceiling ball attempt, the returner would most certainly be out of position for the next shot.

There are, however, moments when the garbage serve can be returned in a more pleasurable fashion. It involves playing a game of cat and mouse with the server, but the reward is worth the effort.

Cognizant that garbage serves tend to be returned to the ceiling the server will calmly hit another garbage your way. Instead of readying the predictable return, run forward with haste. If you can meet the ball in the air before it bounces, (remember the 5-foot line) you're

Ceiling ball return is the logical answer to garbage and Z-ball serves.

orbiting around three walls (from side-to-front-to-side) and watch the fun.

The change in tactics should provoke an immediate, and highly visible reaction from the server, especially if he or she is a newcomer. Instead of floating leisurely towards the backwall as in response to the ceiling ball, the server must think quickly.

"Where's the ball going to land?" is a question likely to spring into mind. Despite the laws of physics preventing the sphere from traveling anywhere but center court, the server is likely to have forgotten. Focusing intently on the ball's flight he may take a series of short, disjointed jumps around center-court. This motion will benefit the returner greatly after the ball touches down. While many claim the sight of the server emulating a jumping bean is a winner in its own right, the ensuing loss of position can prove as costly. Off-balance and puzzled as to the ball's destination, the server is faced with two choices. Either try to hit the ball in mid-air, a difficult volley at best, or play the shot off the bounce. That's no easy feat in itself, as the ball will tend to angle directly towards the back corner. In order to make the shot the server will have to turn around and try to bisect the angle from behind. Obviously this is not an easy maneuver to execute. It is, however, possible—a fact we'll discuss in our later discussion of unique shots.

So, used at the right time, the a-t-w-b can be a productive ally in the battle against the garbage serve.

Some Additional Thoughts

There will be times, albeit few in number, the returner comes face-to-face with a lob serve. If the tricky effort is executed properly, there's not much else to do but send the orb roofward. You can also choose to employ the a-t-w-b if the mood strikes you. In either case, there are a few things to look for before acting.

Every time a lob serve is delivered the server is flirting with danger. The ball may rebound off the back wall, or fail to glance off the side wall before landing. In either case, the result should read plum. Prior to launching any of the recommended returns study the serve carefully—it could go badly for the server, and that means good news for you.

Any readers who are interested in the serve return may wonder why the a-t-w-b wasn't listed as a return for the Z-serve. Here's an attempt to address the issue.

The a-t-w-b can be used as a return in this case, but beginners tread carefully. It's one thing to inform a player about the zig-zag path of the serve, and another to ask it be returned in kind. At first sighting the two wall contact and puzzling bounce of the Z-serve can trouble a newcomer. To require the same individual to respond by lashing the ball back off three walls seems a bit much early in the game.

Once the player has become attuned to the proclivities of the Z-serve, however, there's nothing wrong with a lusty a-t-w-b every now and then.

entitled to the cheese. All that remains is for you to rivet a hard drive before he or she has time to react. This won't be hard to do, as the server will probably be totally surprised by the maneuver. Since you'll be but a few feet behind it should be no problem to whistle a V-pass by. Disaster can strike though, if you choose to hit down the line and the server has time to move over.

At this stage some readers are bound to ask, "What about the around-the-wall-ball for a return?" When dealing with the garbage and lob serve, it should be considered a strong possibility. Especially when the garbage serve is traveling at about chest height and you're eager for a change of pace. Trusty allies like the ceiling ball should always be appreciated, but there are moments when a note of diversity is called for. What should you do, though, when the serve coming towards you rules against a drive? Why step up, send the ball

The curse of the impatient! 1—
Rally begins with a garbage serve
to the backhand corner. 2—A
down-the-line ceiling ball follows
from the returner. 3—The players
switch center court position as
another ceiling ball is returned to

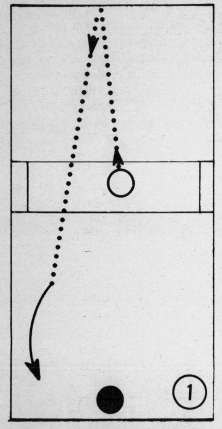

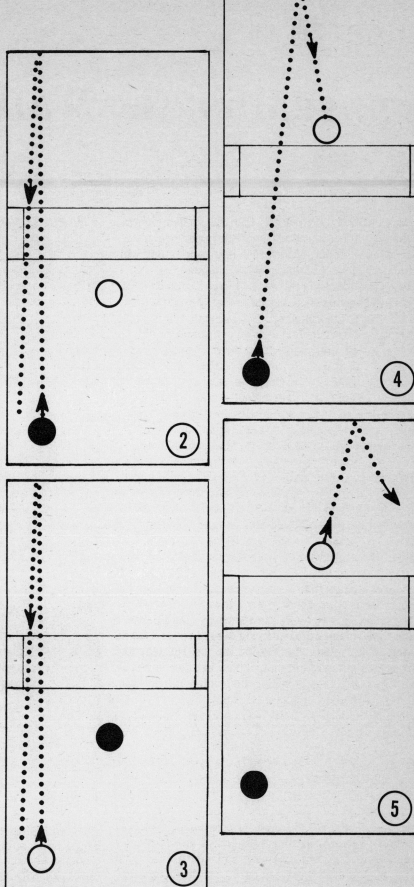

the same area. 4—Growing impatient, the returner tries a
crosscourt drive to the forehand
side. 5—The shot is not hit properly, and the defender is in perfect
position for a straight-wall kill.

CHAPTER 15

Up Against the Wall(s)

IT WAS MENTIONED EARLIER that an examination of the off-the-back-wall kill would be included at a later date. Well, that part of the prose is at hand, along with some other facets of wall play in general.

Prior to addressing the issue of back wall kills it can be helpful to dwell on the nature of the walls themselves. Although composed of hard materials such as cement the walls should never be considered an adversary. Granted, there will be occasions when parts of the anatomy are thrust into the walls. There will also be occasional rendezvous between racquet and walls. While these confrontations may impart a bruise to flesh, aluminum or fiberglass, the long-term relationship should prove enduring. One of the most important concepts a player can grasp is that the walls can be a friend.

Upon developing instincts that will gradually govern court play, the player will rely on the back and sidewalls more and more. In fact, some of the most enjoyable shots are likely to be bullets shot off the back wall. The sides will become allies in the pursuit of a return, or provide a forward boost to a lagging shot. It's both imperative and enjoyable for the novice to learn to survive and thrive in the field of wall play.

One of the first things a beginner or novice should do upon entering the court is walk towards a side wall. Take a step or two away, turn sideways, and face the front wall. Imagine the ball flying toward you and take a swing at the sphere. Let's hope the test run whistled through to completion. But, if you halted the stroke midway due to an imminent collision with the wall you've learned an important lesson.

When dealing with sidewall shots never approach so closely that the wall impedes the progress of the racquet. Be sure to position yourself far enough away so there is sufficient room to step towards the ball, swing and follow through. All that's required to master this process is some practice.

Proper distance can be roughly computed by standing close to the wall, racquet arm extended, with the racquet edge making contact. Move towards mid-court about three-quarters of a step and you'll have your fail-safe point—or near enough not to have to worry about a showdown.

Above and opposite page—Off-the-wall kill begins with setup (1) where you think ball will come off the back wall. Step into shot (2) as ball begins to pass by. Study ball's speed (3) and begin strong level swing. Contact should be made between knee and ankle range (4) with wrist snap. Follow through (5) with eyes still on point of contact.

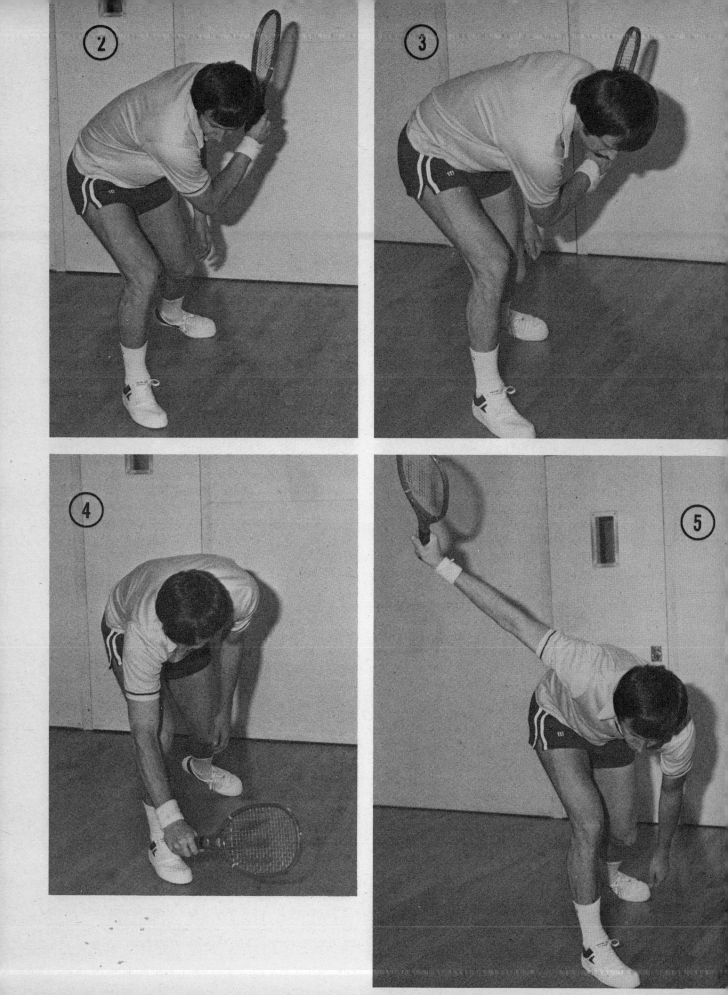

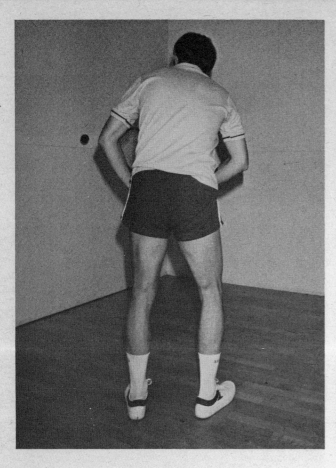

Now that you've hopefully lowered the potential fear quotient concerning sidewall confrontations let's turn to the backwall. Playing a ball off the backwall is a prospect few newcomers relish. This may be prompted by games witnessed where players flailed wildly and unsuccessfully at balls rebounding off the back barrier.

Since the shot most beginners would love to emulate is the off-the-back-wall-kill, let's begin the courtship.

To begin, appearances can be deceiving. Based on an observer's first impression the ability to smite a kill off the backwall seems a god-given-gift. To the untrained eye the shot appears contrary to the norm, as the ball approaches the player from the rear. Moving in concert with the ball in a learned choreography the player adjusts and turns the oddity to his advantage.

But before you can dance, you need to know the steps.

For purposes of studying the off-the-wall-kill, consider the ball and your body as dance partners. The first, and most fundamental step concerns distance. It may seem unorthodox (unless you're a lover of disco) but try to remain at least 2-3 feet from your partner as it (the ball) hits the rear wall. Line up sideways to your dance partner's (the orb's) path, and prepare yourself for an ordinary forehand drive. Watch your partner closely. As it starts to pass by enroute to the front wall step into it with a strong, level swing. After the back wall rebound the ball may come off at a rather low

height. Be sure to make contact between knee and ankle range. If you've carried through the normal techniques of wrist snap, and weight transfer the ball should move fast and low towards the front wall. Keep in mind you have a host of possible kills that can be attempted. Depending on your opponent's position, don't hesitate to shoot a straight down-the-line, midcourt, cross-court, or pinch to either corner.

The off-the-back-wall-kill can quickly become the beginner's best friend. One of the reasons is that newcomers tend to hit their shots too hard. As a result a good number of otherwise competent passes and overheads make unscheduled rebounds off the back wall.

Armed with this knowledge the resourceful novice can put the off-the-back-wall-kill to good use. Terrorizing fellow newcomers as the shooter grows accustomed to gauging the bounce off the back wall, the kills-to-follow can be an exercise in pleasure.

The reason so few players initially warm to the shot is one of the best kept secrets in the game. When you stop to consider it, players are forced to make a host of judgments before *any* return. Where to stand, what shot to try, where is the opponent positioned, etc. On most of these efforts the ball is screaming, lofting, or angling toward the hitter prompting a quick reaction. The tables are turned when the ball takes that hop off the back wall. Anytime the hitter is stationed where he can follow the ball to the backwall the advantage is in hand. By

Opposite page and below—Off-the-wall shot can also be made by moving in tandem with the ball. Taking two or three steps with the ball can add momentum to the shot.

planting your body in the appropriate area before the rebound you can enjoy a moment of unhurried thought.

The player is aware how hard the ball will bounce off the wall (the harder the shot the more forceful the carom) and the path it will follow. A furtive glance forward will reveal the whereabouts of the opposition. With this data in hand all that remains is to marshal the fundamentals and stroke the shot.

Since there's so much time to prepare for the ball's arrival, you can really work on the power potential. By getting the backswing in gear early and tightly recoiling the hips, the shot can be delivered with murderous efficiency. The only problem is that like all things worth possessing, the attainment process is far from quick developing. In other words, it takes practice.

By the way more than a kill can be shot off the back wall. Don't forget about your other weapons. Just gauge the height and speed of the rebound and route your shot accordingly. Remember that you're in a potentially aggressive position whenever you field an off-the-back-wall-ball. Therefore, work on making the return a winner. Steer clear from ceiling balls and the like unless you're off-balance, or you totally lack faith in your low game. If the latter is the case proceed post haste to practice afterwards.

Don't restrict these off-the-wall efforts totally to the forehand. Many of the top players most effective shots are fast-moving drives and kills from the backhand side.

In fact, due to the extension of the racquet arm away from the body, a backhand drive can often be hit harder than its forehand counterpart.

Now that we've covered the basics it's time to dig a little deeper. Some readers are bound to have been eyewitnesses to another style of backwall play. If you're reasonably certain you've seen such an approach, you're right. There is another method of unleashing off-the-wall burners but it can be tricky for new learners.

Whereas it was suggested above to take a position away from the ball, another school of thought exists. Adherents believe more momentum and power can be derived by waltzing with the ball (remember the dance partner analogy) as it departs from the back wall. Using the same stroke as above, the hitter is able to take a step or two enroute to the shot. Therefore the body has that much more time to coil and unwind as it chaperones the ball. To tell the truth, this procedure works, and effectively. The problem is that newcomers often find it difficult to follow the ball. While in the former procedure they are able to stop, setup and wait, the latter causes them to move in tandem with the ball.

Inexperienced players can easily misjudge the ball's speed and height. When this occurs they are forced to lunge, throwing the body off-balance. Sometimes the ball can be misjudged so badly the swing will miss entirely.

Left, above and below—Practice off-the-back wall shots by throwing ball off wall, waiting for it to approach and stepping into shot. Practice kills and drives from forehand and backhand.

There's a means however, to achieve the best of both styles. Newcomers are advised to begin by setting up and awaiting the ball. Once the technique has been mastered the player can confidently employ the second method. After the fundamentals have been grasped the player may prefer the second course of action. If you find one style works better stick with it. Remember the cardinal rule, whatever works is the way to go.

One last point worth noting. Don't expect every shot that caroms off the back wall to float directly towards you. Depending on how hard and high a particular shot is stroked, rebounds can differ wildly in appearance. Some may fail to spring out far from the wall, while others may pulse 15 feet frontward. Whatever the case, be prepared to adjust your setup for the shot. After playing awhile you'll "know" just about how far out a certain shot will rebound and place yourself accordingly.

These off-the-back-wall shots can be fun to practice. Place yourself about 2-3 feet from the back wall and throw a ball off it. Wait for the ball to approach your position and step into the shot. Practice hitting kills and drives from various stations on court. Be sure to repeat the drills from both the forehand and backhand side.

If the bug hits you to try out the waltzing method, practice is the time to do so. Make sure though the change in technique doesn't impede your velocity or consistency.

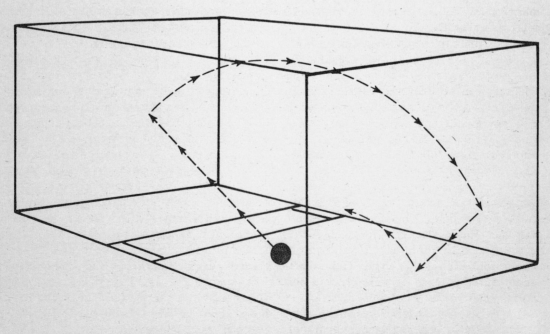

Flight path of a typical front wall to back wall shot.

CHAPTER 16

Twice as Much Fun

DOUBLES IS A VERSION of racquetball currently caught in a maelstrom of controversy. Many singles players are leery of the paired game. They feel there are too many players on the court, hence an increased chance of injury. The charge is made the game is played at too slow a pace and this allows players to hide weaknesses. Others feel a player's strengths can be negated due to the presence of an extra racquet on the defense.

Adherents of doubles are equally vocal in trumpeting positive aspects of play. The game is more strategic in nature, stresses beneficial attributes of team play, and affords a somewhat less strenuous but still extensive workout.

Aside from actual aspects of play this faction also advocates the sociability of doubles, and the decreased expense spread among participants.

All things considered, doubles stands up well to criticism. The game is fun to play and caters to many individuals. Some may lack the time to hone their skills sufficiently for singles play. Others are drawn to the less strenuous pace and increased personal interaction.

Still, don't think all singles players turn thumbs down on doubles. Many top players enjoy the game as an opportunity to refine skills, work on weaknesses, and experiment with strategy.

Before rushing off with a threesome of friends and start playing, there are several differences you should be aware of. Some are glaringly visible to anyone who has ever witnessed a doubles game. Staring onto a court the viewer notices a mass of whirling bodies, flashing racquets, and lengthy rallies. At times it appears a miracle that no damage is inflicted upon the participants. Shots directed wallward seem to have to bypass a human checkerboard to reach the target.

Returns appear equally difficult due to intervening torsos between racquet and ball. Still a definite standard of courtesy can be observed oncourt. This protocol is necessary for pleasurable play and is not learned the first time out. In order for a foursome to engage in a well-played contest the old saw of "safety first" must be sharpened and re-sharpened. Fortunately provisions exist that make the task simple and

permit doubles to be an exciting experience.

Before analyzing the game any further here's a brief runthrough of its distinguishing characteristics.

In case you've wondered, doubles is the reason those boxes are drawn on either side of the service zone. They're there for safety and help insure a burden-free return of service. When a team is serving (point scoring is identical to singles) the server's partner must stand in one of the two boxes. He isn't permitted to exit the box until the ball has passed the short line in flight. From that moment on all systems are go and the rally is on.

Since there are so many players oncourt it's mandatory each refrain from taking undue advantage. Players must strive to allow opponents as clear sight lines as possible. They should also do their best to provide as much room as possible for the opposition to stroke the ball. Undue closeness can lead to bad feelings, botched shots, or worse, a meeting of rubber and flesh. A foursome able to operate within this common-sense framework will become beneficiaries of countless hours of enjoyable doubles.

Once play begins there are several basic strategies that can be employed. With four players it's imperative each member of each team know the whereabouts of his teammate. To facilitate joint awareness and improve play, two different formations can be used. They are known as the side-by-side and "I" formations. Little mystique surrounds either approach—in the former court coverage is divided by sides; in the latter, one player handles front court, the other back court. These procedures are hardly inviolate, however. Any time a player is caught out of position the partner should move to cover the area. As such, considerable random movement is allowed with each approach.

Before delving deeper into the side-by-side or I it's necessary to study how a doubles team is composed. Ideally speaking, the dream team would be composed of a left- and right-handed player. With the southpaw patrolling the left side of the court and the righty the other, the opposition would be unable to attack a vulnerable backhand. Naturally, a side-by-side strategy would be used by this twosome.

Even though lefties are a valuable premium (that's

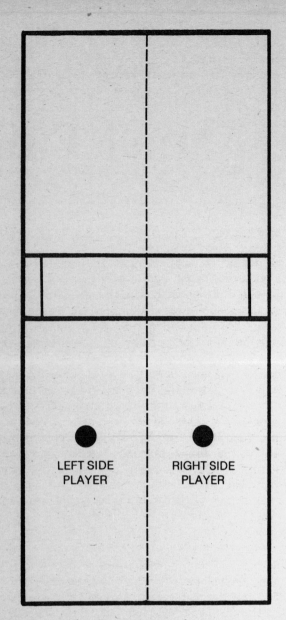

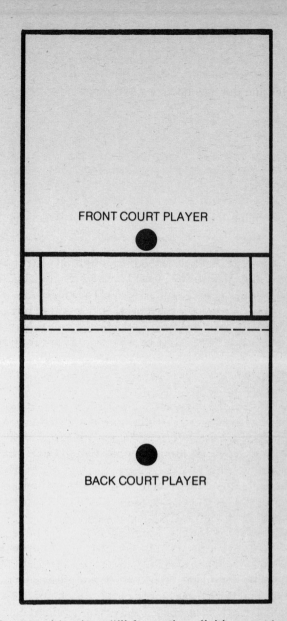

Side-by-side doubles formation divides court coverage into left and right halves.

Front-and-back or "I" formation divides court coverage into front and back halves.

for all the southpaws who have had to bear the onus of substitution throughout this text), most teams are comprised of righties. In this context teams preferring the side-by-side formation place the player with the superior backhand on the left. This alignment also takes care of jurisdictional disputes concerning shots up the middle. Since the player to the left has his or her forehand facing the middle that's who handles the chore.

As a rule far more teams favor the side-by-side than the I style. The reasons are self-evident. First, the player up front in the I must be exceptionally quick in order to cover the front against two opponents. In fact when a front wall rally ensues against a team playing a side-by-side the action can appear lopsided. The side-by-siders will alternate hitting the ball to either side of the front person in the I. Since the rear member remains

in the backcourt the front player must move from one side to the other to make the returns.

After several rallies of this nature, fatigue and frustration can begin to set in. Another negative factor of the I is the issue of jurisdiction. Many times the front man will jump high to return a shot that rightfully belongs to the back court player. Other times the back man may long for some diversity concerning shot selection. While the front player is largely responsible for a good share of kills and volleys the back member is the defensive stalwart. As such the repertoire consists largely of ceiling and high Z-balls. After a while a constant diet of these can become boring. Teams composed of newcomers and veterans alike have also been known to suffer from the overall compatibility blues, regardless of the formation. There's another aspect which can be touched upon. It has to do with the headwork involved in scoring as many points as possible. It's time to deal with strategy, and at this time the difference between singles and doubles becomes extremely noticeable.

Doubles Strategy

Success in singles hinges on a player uncovering and exploiting the weakness of the opposition. Regardless of a player's skill level the sole member of the opposition has the opportunity to analyze every phase of his or her game.

That being the case singles players often employ a strategy of compensation, trying to offset what could be a fatal flaw. In doubles it's nowhere as easy to isolate and capitalize on a weakness. For example, by using a side-by-side attack a player's weak backhand may be protected to the maximum. Poor ratings in footspeed and quickness are also minimized due to lesser coverage responsibilities. Finally, a shot that would be a sure winner in singles often comes to rest on the racquet face of an opponent in doubles.

"If that's the case," you ask, "what's the key to success?" The answer is succinct and compact—*patience*. The team that wins is the crew more willing to play a ceiling game and dominate center court position. The moment the opposition falters the winning twosome is ready to move in quickly for the kill—and kill shot.

Broken down to its essentials, a doubles game resembles an exercise in center court ballet. The team which has just hit strives to move into center court position. After the return has been made the opposition attempts the same. While this practice will not always be observed it sets the tone for an ebb and flow towards center court.

Since rules concerning hinders demand the opposition be given every chance to see and hit the return play becomes very stylized. Both teams therefore seek to minimize errors in search of a long-term lease on center court.

Following these cautious dictates, play inevitably is dominated by the ceiling ball. This makes good sense for another reason. Since both members of the returning team only have to cover a specific area they can become more offensive-minded. Players whose forehands face the side wall can often be seen drooling in anticipation of riveting a poor serve wallward. To defend against this possibility the server works on making the return difficult. Serves tend to be Z's or garbage strokes that force the returner deep into the corner. Confined to that cumbersome area there's little to do but opt for the ceiling ball. Once the ball is lofted skyward the ballet begins.

Keep in mind the rationale for wanting to control center court. If the returning side can be made to stroke their shots from deep court the serving team can seize

"I" formation during doubles game—note that the formation zones are not inviolate. Any time a player is caught out of position, the partner should move to cover the area.

center court position. Stationed thusly they can await a mistake and attack aggressively with low drives, passes and kills. By the way, beginners should be aware few points are won on the service. So work on placing your serves deep. Always try to concentrate your attack on the weaker player. Since most teams will use the side-by-side formation this effort can be easily implemented.

Whenever possible stroke shots that will exploit the lesser player's deficits. This tactic will accomplish several goals: it will cause the player under attack to press, become self-conscious and try to overcompensate. The player's mate will likely tire of being excluded and exceed his or her territorial imperative. As soon as the superior player vacates a side of play, direct the attack to the open area. By stroking the ball towards an uncovered region points should be reaped and tempers made to flare.

The opposition will be left somewhat puzzled. Is it wiser to have both players defending against a particular problem, or allow one to fare miserably? The question is one most doubles teams owning the service would love to face.

Another profit-yielding approach stresses the diversity of tempo. During the heat of a game your team may sense the other side seems to be attuned to your playing wavelength. Whenever the thought arises exchange a few words with your partner and begin mixing things up.

Serve to the opposite side more often, use more of a certain type of pass than before, etc. Sometimes the very change of pace can reap bonuses for your side.

Games featuring beginners can often be bewildering experiences for both players and spectators. The necessary courtesies between teams aren't always extended, with expected results. Denied clear sight lines for down-the-line, pinch shots, kills and crosscourt passes, players will shoot with impaired accuracy. With no air traffic controller available to channel the flow the ball will make many unscheduled landings on opposition backs.

These ill-conceived touchdowns create attention on two levels. The primary reaction is one of surprise on the part of the player who has just been pelted. This surprise only lasts a second however, as a stinging sensation takes over. While the pain alone is sufficient to prompt fear of future occurrences the worst is yet to come. It's the slow birth of a red circular welt, better suited for use on a griddle. Fortunately with time the red pancake subsides, but the after-effects may linger. After being struck at close range the hittee may experience some ill-will towards the hitter.

Since racquetball is a game of civilized men and women, such actions as fisticuffs rarely come to the fore. More likely, the player who has been welted may become suspicious and gunshy as the game continues. If the incident transpires again a good chance exists the participants will fail to engage in post-game festivities.

In fact, an individual given to branding opponents might find it difficult to drum up a partner.

With increased court time the majority of newcomers readily adapt to the constraints and strategic differences of doubles. Once the fundamentals have been mastered the game can become a haven for the totally competitive but no more than marginally skilled. Played properly doubles can take the form of a chess match, with each team attacking and waiting, attacking and waiting, until the 21st point has been scored.

Couples also find doubles attractive. It allows mates to compete with and against each other in a pleasurable fashion. Differences in proficiency are overcome by different pairings, such as the least with the most able.

One last note, remember the team that controls center court should be the aggressor. Work towards dominating this position and you'll find there's a lot more to doubles than a ceiling game.

By the way, there's a difference regarding the service you must be aware of. The first time the ball is put in play only one player gets to serve. When a rally is lost the returning team takes over, with each member serving in turn. At the next change both members of the original service team are granted a serve. So, when you step oncourt for a doubles game remember: the service rule, to stay in the service box until the serve passes the short line, and be courteous. Carry out these two dictums and you're bound to have twice the fun.

The Game of Cutthroat

Occasionally the situation will develop when one of your foursome is unable to make it. What happens then? Do you play one against two, singles, or call the game off? Neither. Before you can say "What's left?", here's the answer: Cutthroat. No, it's not an attempt to incite two of the threesome against the other. It's a game designed for three players which incorporates aspects of both singles and doubles.

The game begins with one of the participants serving while the other two function as a doubles team. Putting the ball in play the server does his or her best to win the rally. Points are scored in the regular fashion. When the doubles team manages to win a rally the player on the left-hand side takes over the service. The former server moves to the right-hand doubles position, while the player in that spot moves to the left. Play continues to rotate until one player becomes the first to score 21 points.

Cutthroat is interesting inasmuch as the singles player stands an excellent chance to defeat the pair if they don't play as a team. As the scoring begins to build, a player's loyalties are subject to shift with each new doubles combination.

While it's a world of fun, players should realize with the serve constantly changing it can take time to play a game. Enough time perhaps to drum up a fourth for doubles.

CHAPTER 17

On the Attack

TODAY'S RACQUETBALLER is predominately offense-minded. This stands to reason as the kill, low drive and rollout are the game's prime attention getters. A problem encountered by many newcomers is a lack of awareness concerning how to employ the offensive weapons they've been developing.

Strategically speaking, offensive racquetball is based on a theory of attack at the opportune moment. In order to be able to exploit that moment it's necessary to understand the concept of center court position.

The player dominating the area from the middle of the service zone to a yard or two behind the short line should be in the driver's seat. Situated anywhere in this region he or she should be able to control the flow of play, make life difficult for the opposition, and easily reach most returns.

Naturally the server enjoys the initial opportunity to establish center court dominance. If the serve (which is decidedly an offensive weapon) is cleverly delivered the returner should find it hard to answer in kind. Ready and waiting, the server should pounce on a weak return for a winner. How to best do it? Several approaches can be recommended.

When serving do your utmost to hit the ball to the opposition's backhand. This will minimize your opponent's usage of the forehand, probably the other side's most effective stroke.

If the return comes in the form of a weak flutter ball knee-high or above use a crisp drive to win the point. A cross-court would be appropriate if the opponent has remained on the backhand side. A down-the-line version is called for if the foe has raced too far towards the forehand side. Be sure to stroke this shot down the backhand line.

What if the return of serve comes low off the front wall? A kill or very low drive is in order. Check the returner's position and act accordingly. If he or she remains stuck in the backhand corner tap a low drive to the forehand side (make sure the shot doesn't kick off the side wall after the front wall contact). By the same standard a side-front-wall pinch to the backhand side would also prove effective. Glancing off the side wall the ball would strike the front wall and bounce low

Whenever the hitter is able to assume such devastating command of the center court position the opposition will be hard pressed to respond.

across the court. With the opponent far from front court it would be an exceptionally difficult return.

The opponent may not always be trapped deep in the backcourt after returning your serve. If that's the case, but the return still leaves a great deal to be desired, think lower. Utilize either of the returns mentioned above, but hit kill shots. Due to the increased velocity and lower height a nearby opponent should still be out of contention.

Any time you're presented with a clearcut opportunity for a kill be sure to evaluate the opposition. There's nothing more embarrassing than hitting a kill directly to the wrong place.

The majority of serves, however, will probably be

Left—Evaluate your opposition before unleashing a kill. A ceiling ball launched from deep is a far better bet than hitting a kill to the wrong place.

Below—After making a shot, reclaim center court and wait for your opponent to commit a mental or physical error.

returned in a competent fashion. Most times they will take the form of ceiling balls. When faced with a sky-high return step briskly back and await the descent. When the ball comes close stroke another ceiling ball, preferably to the backhand side, and move forward.

Reclaim center court position and wait for your opponent to commit a mental or physical error. Don't be afraid to engage in prolonged ceiling play. No game was ever discontinued because of an endless ceiling rally. Once again, work at maintaining center court position and wearing the other side down.

Constantly look for weaknesses though, and attack the instant one appears. By the way, be careful when launching assaults, especially in regard to the kill shot. Keep in mind a pass will often work as well with a minimum of risk. Work on recognizing your range of effectiveness with the kill and venture beyond sparingly. Most players have increasing success as they approach closer and closer towards the front wall. It's a fact worth retaining next time you prepare to unleash a

35-foot rollout. Generally speaking, shoot your kills from about the 15- 25-foot range whenever possible. Of course there will be moments ripe for the likes of an off-the-back-wall-kill. When such moments arrive, hit the shot with confidence.

The Mental Side of Offense

Another important consideration has to do with the score, and who's serving. Pressure tends to bite deepest when the score is close. Many competitors begin to wilt when the game is knotted. Keep in mind you're the only one aware of your internal disposition.

Regardless of your offensive skills always try to play within the bounds of your temperament. If you feel the tension beginning to take hold when you're faced with a choice of valid shots, opt for the easier way. It may do your ego a world of good to smoke a kill off the front wall, but a miss could prove disastrous to the psyche. On the other hand with increased play you should expand your shotmaking capability. With the accompany-

Below—Sometimes a competent player will squander a host of opportunities—usually it's due to a reluctance to select shots with an eye for positioning or returnability.

Right—Most players have increasing success with the kill as they approach closer and closer to the front wall.

ing confidence gained enroute a close score is less likely to bring forth future nervous seizures.

Sometimes a highly-skilled player will offensively blunder his way into danger. Blessed with a wicked forehand and backhand, owner of a competent ceiling game, and possessor of a deadly kill, the individual loses more often than not. Why. The answer has nothing to do with physical ability. Players of this ilk are plagued with cerebral short-comings—due to a reluctance to select shots with an eye for positioning or makeability, they squander hordes of opportunities.

While the scenario may not fit your play, it serves as a reminder to keep your thinking cap on. That's why it's important to remember whether you're serving or receiving. When faced with the dilemma of whether to kill or not to kill, mull over the possible results. Given a difficult shot such as an off-the-backwall-kill consider the result of an unsuccessful attempt. If the service is lost the score remains the same; if a point is sacrificed you're one step closer to defeat.

Impatience may dictate you to ponder another alternative. There will be games when you're so far out of contention there's nothing to lose. Fire away on all fronts and hope for a series of miracles. If you're lucky, a rollout or two may grace your racquet, causing the opposition to wonder. Given a generous balance of continued good fortune and poor play by the opponent you may remain in contention.

Chances are, however, an all-out kill strategy will put the last nails in the coffin. So what, at least you'll have gone down blazing.

On the other extreme, it's a good gamble to overkill when you're on top of the score by a big margin and serving.

The worst that can happen is the service will switch hands. You can still play an aggressive defense as the opponent is likely to be pressing. Upon regaining the service a few accurate kills and drives should add up to victory.

CHAPTER 18

The Inner & Outer Player

THE TIME SPAN will vary with each player but eventually the bulk of the strokes will be mastered. Eager to flash these hard-to-come-by skills more than a few newcomers will seek out fresh blood in the form of different competitors. Removed from the comfortable arena of playing against the same few individuals the game will take on a different perspective.

Whereas good old Joe or Joan is aware of your every flaw and you theirs, a strange face in the service box is unaware of your shortcomings. Unfortunately many beginners fail to realize the opposition is equally ignorant of your assets. Whenever you engage an opponent for the first time remember he may be every bit as terrified by your intimidating stature (or at least your nerveless facade). The key to success is to be totally honest with yourself as to your strengths and weaknesses, and how they can be applied to favorable advantage.

Any competitor you face will either be visibly superior, inferior, or roughly equal to you in talent. Unless of course you choose to flex your fledgling talents against the club or area champion (even then however, all may not be lost). It can be extremely helpful to formulate certain strategies which can be calmly and readily applied—depending on the competition.

Racquetball players can generally be sorted into categories, in which they participate with varying degrees of effectiveness. Despite any fears you may be harboring there are few players short of the professional ranks who qualify as four-walled Renaissance Men (or Women).

There will be times when you enter the court and come upon an opponent able to make the ball travel as if it were an Intercontinental Ballistic Missile. Warming up alongside this juggernaut it's an easy matter to be quickly and fatally intimidated.

Observe the opposition thoroughly and consider whether or not he or she has a wide range of weapons ready for use. Chances are good when play is initiated that the big gun is the only armament available. From the first service the opponent has pinned hopes for victory on the ability to leave you quaking in the wake of a wicked forehand drive. To paraphrase a sage, forewarned is forearmed. Instead of conceding a barrage of points and rallies to the speeding rubber comet turn the deficit to your advantage.

Base your attack on a succession of ceiling balls and high-Z's. Forced to retreat to deep backcourt for returns the opponent will be stretching the accuracy of the speeding bullet to the breaking point. Low drives and kills that scored as winners from the 15-25-foot range will suddenly and abruptly come up short.

Passes that whizzed by too fast to be seen clearly (let alone be returned) will spend more time inflight. Make sure to stroke a majority of your rooftoppers and anglers to the backhand side. Many practitioners of the forehand alone school have surprisingly weak backhands. They are able to mask the inadequacy by the force of their forehand bludgeon. The thought and act of having to demonstrate a functional backhand can often rend their game asunder. Given a certain amount of patience on your part the overhead route should reap dividends. Once the opponent becomes sufficiently unnerved the one-track game plan will falter. Anxious to achieve redemption the individual may begin to attack with even more ferocity, and less aim.

Strategically positioned in center court you should have little trouble turning these hot shots into cool points.

While this strategy can prove effective it is contingent on two points. First, your ceiling game must be developed to the degree it can provide an adequate irritant. Second, you must always assume center court position as your opponent retreats for the return. There's another pleasant offshoot from the fruitful application of this theory of disarmament. The more setups the heavy hitter returns, the defter your kill shot and passing game will appear. By the time the 21st point is scored the would-be intimidator may walk off the court feeling beaten by a master. If only he or she really knew the truth.

Other games will match you against a far more competent brand of opponent—a player who not only can hit hard but possesses a wide repetoire of strokes and shots. Or to put it bluntly, a superior racquetball player. What

One theory for victory against a better opponent is to play the percentages and hope that the foe will falter—a ceiling game works well here.

should you do? Concede defeat and plead a forgotten appointment? Play a point or two and suddenly sprain an ankle? Maybe even bash your racquet against the wall and render it useless? Hardly. What's needed is the ability to play a guerilla-warfare type of game.

Watch Your Enemy

No matter how skillful the opponent may be it stands to reason some facets of his game are better than others. If you take time to watch carefully during the warmup you may be able to isolate such an area. If so, move to exploit it. If not, there are two tacks worthy of pursuit.

The first is based on the principle of the cobra: strike first. The other on the fable of the tortoise and the hare: stall for time and make the other guy play your game.

Let's examine the former. Even though the opposition may be better that's not to say you should think less of your assets. Rely extensively on your strength whether it be defensive or offensive. As soon as possible strike for the proverbial jugular. Once you establish the ability to duel with the foe on at least one level (the ceiling game for example) a certain amount of respect should appear. A respect not necessarily limited to recognizing your proficiency. Striving to wipe

away your measure of competency the opponent may play in a predictable, easily fathomed fashion. As soon as you are reasonably aware of what the return will be, think points. You may come up short for a while but the attacking strategy should cause your opponent to approach with caution. If the kill has been your strong point, shoot it with confidence. Perhaps you've had luck (or avoided disaster) with the low drive. In that case hit it just a little harder and alter the direction. Your shots may not be etched into the annals of the game but they may score a quick point or two. Sure, the odds remain stacked against you, but they're by no means mountain high. In fact, if you're able to keep the heat on with a combination of your best skills and surprise the game could turn around.

Psychology plays a big part in any game or match, and a little mental oneupmanship can only aid your cause. At worst you'll have bowed to a superior player; but he will have known he's been in a game. And what more could a beginner ask for?

The other theory for victory against insurmountable odds is much less daring. It entails playing the percentages and hoping the opposition will falter. This avenue is employed by relying on an overhead game to prolong each rally. Optimism is predicated on the hope the opponent will seek to make fast work of you. Therefore it follows (but only barely) he will make the wrong shot at the right time. Namely launch an epidemic of fullcourt kills that will fall short or go astray. Then again your opponent may choose to react to the monotony with a slew of exotic shots, in the notion that the wizardry may baffle you and stifle your ceiling game.

Frankly speaking neither of these events will happen often. When they do, you may be so surprised by the tactic that you're unable to convert the plums into winners—this lack of aggressiveness is fatal.

This is not to say that a ceiling game is in any way a poor strategy to utilize against more skilled opponents. Without the desire to follow up an opponent's miscues with offensive attacks it is, however, rendered impotent.

It wouldn't be fair to convey the idea each time you step oncourt you're going to encounter an awesome gladiator. The skills you possess may prove sufficient at times to easily carry you to victory. During such confidence building encounters it's important to ensure you don't become your own worst enemy. The notion that your ability is more than adequate to subdue an opponent is often the first step to defeat. Enthralled with the vision of riveting kill after kill you, the "favorite," may try to put the dream into practice.

Confident of being able to deal with any threat mounted by the obviously inferior foe you, the "killer", run wild about court. Impatient to wrap up the game, thoughts of center court position and percentage shots vanish in a bloodthirsty haze. As the would-be-assassin begins to fall prey to avarice the thought of defeat

Strive to exploit an opponent's weaknesses. Here a tendency to delay in returning serves is attacked with a drive serve.

becomes a fearful spectre. Unwilling to come to terms with the need for a change in strategy the self-induced carnage continues.

Finally, as the supposed inferior walks off victorious, you, the "loser" can be glimpsed off in a corner, muttering. It's impossible to relate your exact words, but they all sound about the same. "How did I ever manage to blow the game? Well, I'll really wipe him (or her) off the court next time." What you should have thought is, "That's what happens when I play with my heart instead of my head."

How should you attack a weaker player? It all depends on the weakness. The majority of players, regardless of experience, tend to have backhands that are weaker than their forehands. To combat the frailty these individuals rely on a strong forehand, a competent ceiling game and excellent speed afoot. Once uncovered however, the backhand liability should be exploited.

When it becomes evident the opponent is favoring the forehand and running around the backhand, take charge. Begin to hit the majority of shots to the backhand side, preferably deep. Forced into the corner the opposition will find the lack of acreage poses a

problem. Without enough room to maneuver past the backhand there's no choice but to launch it. The effort will usually bring forth piteous results. While the opponent's forehand may resemble a firecracker, and his ceiling game is a creature of respect, the backhand inspires only giggles. Drives arch high onto the front wall, victims of an overly exposed racquet face. Attempted kills fall into the floorboards well short of the mark. The cause of their demise: an overly closed racquet face. Backhand ceiling balls fare no better. Oozing almost straight upward they contact the ceiling and speed floorwards.

As the opposition's shortcoming becomes more evident, you should strive for winners on shots that exploit his/her weakness. Since the hitter will likely be pinned in the backhand corner it's easy to fire winning crosscourt drives to his forehand side. While it's possible to fire kill shots there's really no need, as the less risky low drive will make do.

You may also run into a player who has trouble getting out of the starting blocks. For one reason or another certain individuals have terrible experiences returning serves. Some are unable to return a drive or Z, while others have trouble with the garbage or lob. When you're matched against such a player the strategy is clearcut. Attack the weakness by serving the serve most hated.

Battling to cope, the opponent will mishit some returns and send occasional weak shots wallward. Those that reach the front wall should be quickly dispatched. Refrain from dishing up the same serve exclusively. Alter the pace with a different service or one hit to the other side. When the opponent is granted the service he will be forced to play catchup, and rely too much on kills and drives.

The Shooting Gallery Syndrome

There are several other shortcomings opponents display that can aid an intelligent player significantly. For reasons somewhat uncertain many players fail to watch the opponent as he returns a shot. A possible cause for this lack of scrutiny may be the shooting gallery syndrome. Turning the head to glance at a return an individual could feel the ball will be hit in his direction—and hard!

Somehow, perhaps due to superstition, the player assumes the ball will not make contact because of the no-peeking tactic. The vast majority of time this lack of foresight will cost the non-looker the rally. Reflexes and anticipation are the keys to successful racquetball. Any player failing to watch a return loses the opportunity to ascertain the opponent's shot selection and direction. Exploit this frailty of the lazy gaze with low drives and kills. Hit the ball with as much power as is practical to cause your opponent's reactions to work overtime.

Stroke as many low Z-balls and around-the-wall ef-

CHAPTER 19

And Then Some

WE'VE NEGLECTED to dwell throughout on the strokes which don't fall into the realm of the orthodox.

One of these is known as the off-the-back-wall-first (o-b-w-f) shot. Honestly speaking, this stroke should never be used except as a last resort. Even then, try to come up with a more palatable alternative.

The need for the shot occurs frequently to newcomers and less often with experience. It's a good thing, as few players enjoy looking like a runaway stork in retreat. Which is as accurate a description as any when evaluating the almost non-shot.

The rarity comes into play when a participant is caught out of position. Stationed near midcourt the soon-to-be-mad-dasher is caught flatfooted as the ball passes overhead. Descending from about 10 feet the ball will bounce and float towards the back wall.

Unfortunately it lacks the power to contact the back wall on the fly. Noting this phenomenon the player is forced into rapid retreat. Rushing back towards the orb the gap between racquet and ball narrows. Finally,

stretched virtually full-length towards the backwall, racquet and ball meet. Taking a mighty swipe the hitter strokes upwards at the ball, hoping to drive it about five feet high off the back wall. The stroke must be executed just right.

Assuming all goes well, the hitter has managed to loft the ball in the direction of the front wall—it should carry clear to the front wall without hitting the floor. Bouncing off the front wall, the ball will land in front of the short line and move to the back court. So far so good. Except, and it's inevitable in this case, the ball will die well before reaching the rear. On most occasions it will never receive the chance to expire. The opposition, positioned in center court in peace while you've been whirling like a dervish, has been following the action.

Racquet at the ready he will intercept the ball roughly waist high. It's hard to describe the return as it will generally be too fast to follow.

The majority of beginners manage to learn to cope

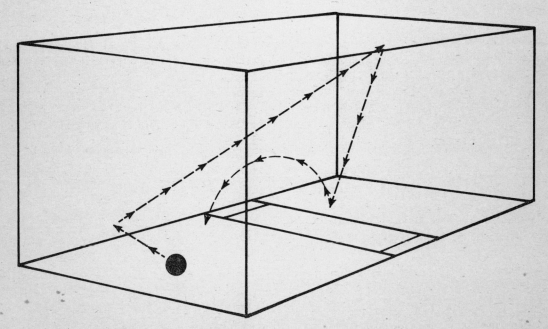

Off-the-back-wall-first shot diagrammed— it's a last resort when caught out of position.

Below and right—The off-the-back-wall-first shot is executed by tracking the ball from behind and stroking it upward toward the back wall.

with the frustration of having to deliver the o-b-w-f shot. Which, incidently can be stroked with equal ineffectiveness with fore- or backhand.

As time goes by tables tend to turn. After a short while (that can seem inexorable) the hopeless scrambler evolves into a clever court-hardened strategist.

In fact, the prospect of returning an o-b-w-f shot looks terrific; while your opponent gyrates towards the backwall.

A Final Note

Judging from the horde of instructional material on the market, many may think the game is exceptionally structured.

Certainly there are matters of fundamental form and shot selection that should be heeded. That's not to say however, racquetball cannot be enjoyed from a free-lance perspective.

There will be moments when hitters will leap into the air, dive toward the floor, and squat in the corner while returning a shot.

Other efforts will stress the less-than-artistic two-handed forehand, limp wristed overhead, and that great favorite, the spastic wrist snap.

Overheads will hit the floor before the front wall; kills will die long before reaching the same.

Although thoughts of this litany of ineptitude are enough to make a first-timer blanch, relax.

If it's true that misery loves company, there's nary a member of the racquetball fraternity who's ever been alone.

At this point stop and reflect on the wide range of individuals who have come to play and love the game. They range from the athletic to the sedentary. The devoted practitioner to the once-a-month dabbler.

Within a week of being introduced to the sport these neophytes can and do compete with reckless abandon. Operating at an initial level of mediocrity, these performers know the joy of wholehearted competition.

Given time the majority become relatively skilled. A smaller but by no means exclusive faction become top players, the toast of their club or facility.

Owing to the unique property of being enjoyed and mastered by the masses, racquetball is growing more popular with each month.

The caliber of play is improving, with more and more newcomers dropping in to give the sport a try.

What more can be asked of a game played in a vault-like room with sawed-off tennis racquets and a soft rubber ball?